0059036

D1061329

DATE DUE

MAR 17 1997

Empire As a Way of Life

Unfortunately, the United States has never
learned to listen to itself as if it were the
enemy speaking.

THOMAS M. FRANCK

AND

EDWARD WEISBAND, 1972.

If you do not acknowledge the reality of the
empire, then the empire goes on without any
moral supervision.

MARTIN GREEN, 1979.

EMPIRE
AS A WAY OF LIFE

An Essay on the Causes
and Character of America's
Present Predicament
Along With a Few Thoughts
About an Alternative

WILLIAM APPLEMAN WILLIAMS

OXFORD UNIVERSITY PRESS
Oxford   New York   Toronto   Melbourne

OXFORD UNIVERSITY PRESS
Oxford   London   Glasgow
New York   Toronto   Melbourne   Auckland
Delhi   Bombay   Calcutta   Madras   Karachi
Kuala Lumpur   Singapore   Hong Kong   Tokyo
Nairobi   Dar es Salaam   Cape Town

and associate companies in
Beirut   Berlin   Ibadan   Mexico City   Nicosia

Library of Congress Cataloging in Publication Data
Williams, William Appleman.
Empire as a way of life.
1. United States—Territorial expansion.
2. United States—Foreign relations.   I. Title.
E179.5.W537   327.73   80-12020   ISBN 0-19-502766-3
ISBN 0-19-503045-1 pbk.

Printing (last digit):   9 8 7

Printed in the United States of America

For
MAUDE HAMMOND APPLEMAN
Witness to the Truth of
Non-Imperial Community

On Defining the Problem

I am persuaded no constitution was never before as well calculated as ours for extensive empire and self-government.

THOMAS JEFFERSON TO JAMES MADISON, April 27, 1809

[Accept a doctrine, and allow it] to go on and grow, you will awaken some day to find it standing over you, the arbiter of your destiny, against which you are powerless, as men are powerless against delusions.

WILLIAM GRAHAM SUMNER, 1903

"Can't repeat the past?" *he cried incredulously.* *"Why of course you can."*

JAY GATSBY, 1925

THE WORDS *empire* and *imperialism* enjoy no easy hospitality in the minds and hearts of most contemporary Americans. That has not always been the case. *Empire* was common to the vocabulary of the Americans who made the revolution against Great Britain, and those who conceived and carried through the subsequent domestic upheaval that replaced the Articles of Confederation with the Constitution.

Those people, our Revolutionary and Founding Fathers, knew the ideas, language, and reality of empire from their study of the classic literature about Greece and Rome (and about politics in general); they used the word regularly in their talk about England; and they came increasingly to employ it in speaking of their own condition, policies, and aspirations. It became, indeed, synonymous with the realization of their Dream—no matter whether they honored the vision of a City on the Hill giving Truth to Mankind, spoke of vast property holdings in the city or on the frontier, sought a tiny clearing in the wilderness, or worried about social and political stability within a framework of representative government.

Later generations became steadily less candid about their imperial attitudes and practices. They talked ever more about "extending the area of freedom," supporting such noble principles as "territorial and administrative integrity," and "saving the world for democracy"—even as they destroyed the cultures of the First Americans, conquered half of Mexico, and relentlessly expanded their government's power around the globe. Empire became so intrinsically our American way of life that we rationalized and suppressed the nature of our means in the euphoria of our enjoyment of the ends. Abundance was freedom, and freedom was abundance. The democratic City on the Hill. Hence we projected our imperium outward upon others—avowed friends as well as damned antagonists.

That process of reification—of transforming the realities of expansion, conquest, and intervention into pious rhetoric about virtue, wealth, and democracy—reached its culmination during the decades after World War II. There are countless documents which monitor the progress of our imperial self-deception, our surrender to doctrine: from a sanctimonious "essay" in *Time* to tough-minded top-secret memoranda about using nerve gas. But perhaps the most illuminating manuscript is the 1949–50 study by the National Security Council known as NSC-68. The leaders of the United States asserted the unique right and responsibility to impose their chosen "order among nations" so that "our free society can flourish."

It was not enough for the United States "merely to seek to check the Kremlin." "Our policy and action," warned NSC-68, "must be such as to foster a fundamental change in the nature of the Soviet system." Any less global imperial policy would have a "drastic effect on our belief in ourselves and in our way of life." Neither the man from the Ivy League nor the once failed haberdasher from Missouri could survive such a trauma. They defined the issue as apocalyptic: the "fulfillment or destruction not only of this Republic but of civilization itself."

The substance of the outlook proved even more impressive than the rhetoric, though the latter was explosive enough in its own right. On the matter of foreign aid (particularly food), the *Wall Street Journal* proudly proclaimed—in one of its typically muddled metaphors—that "we aren't the tooth-fairy handing out sugar plums"; and went on to acknowledge our "cultural imperialism." Policy-makers, intellectuals, and people on Main Street locked minds and marched in protest against losing China, Cuba, and various other societies that we had presumed to own or control in the name of self-determination. Secretary of State Henry Kissinger encapsulated all such imperial evangelicalism in his judgment on intervening to overthrow an *elected* government in Chile. "I don't see why we need to stand by and permit a country to go Communist due to the irresponsibility of its own people."

The reality behind such imperial rhetoric is perhaps most effectively dramatized without reviewing the story of our machinations to "destabilize" an elected government, and without emphasizing our redundant stockpile of nuclear weapons and delivery systems. Consider these mundane vital statistics from the 1970s:

1. Fifty percent of all our scientists and engineers are employed in militarily related work.

2. Fifty-three percent of every federal tax dollar is used to pay for past, present, and anticipated military operations.

3. Federal budget expenditures provide $418 per person for the military, $200 per person for health care, and $32 per person for education.

4. The federal budget does not fund *even one person* whose primary responsibility is to think about stopping and reversing the arms race.

What John Kenneth Galbraith calls "the strategic mind" reigns supreme. It is the imperial mind which looks at a map and divides it "into spheres of present or potential influence." The mind of "a romantic egoist," nicely defined by John K.

Fairbank: "given our patriotic idealism and culture bound insensitivity, if we had not fought in Korea and in Vietnam we would no doubt have fought somewhere else." As indeed we did fight somewhere else. And may well fight again somewhere else.

For we have only just begun our confrontation with our imperial history, our imperial ethic, and our imperial psychology. It is perhaps a bit too extreme, but if so only by a whisker, to say that imperialism has been the opiate of the American people. Drs. Alan D. Forker and Robert S. Eliot put it this way: We have just begun to come to terms with the "fight or flight" psychology that has informed our entire history. We have been nudged to the edge of that confrontation by the energy crisis, but the issue goes far, far beyond the inconvenience of waiting for gasoline and chopping wood for heat.

Perhaps Carll Tucker of the *Saturday Review* put it as well as anyone: "We cannot say no to our desires." But the desires (and the expectations) involved as an inherent part of our imperial way of life, and hence what Haynes Johnson describes as our "growing national disillusionment when it appears that the desires must be limited." Thus it is pointless for President Jimmy Carter to try to rally us with his words about looking "to the future" unless he speaks the truth about the necessity for us to define a non-imperial future.

Even *Time*, that apostle of "The American Century," does better than Carter. The editors say bluntly that America is "a shocking wastrel," that "whole nations could live comfortably on [our] leftovers," and dares even to call for a revival of the ideal of sharing our resources as equals grazing our animals on the ancient Commons. Let us hope we are beginning to nibble at the edges of the problem.

This essay is an effort to move us beyond what *Times* calls "the quibbling stage." A blunt attempt to help us understand and accept our past as an imperial peolple who must now "order" ourselves rather than policing and saving the world. I was born and reared in our American womb of empire, but my experience and my study of history have enabled me to understand that we must leave that imperial incubator if we are to become citizens of the real world. Our future is here and now, a community to be created among ourselves so that we can be citizens—not imperial overlords—of the world.

Jay Gatsby notwithstanding, we cannot repeat the past.

W. A. W.
April 1980

CONTENTS

Empire As a Way of Life

INTRODUCTION

On Disentangling the Threads
of Our Imperial Lifestyle

Everything is related immediately or remotely to every other thing.

JAMES MADISON, 1819

Imperialism has penetrated the fabric of our culture, and infected our imagination, more deeply than we usually think.

MARTIN GREEN,
Dreams of Adventure, Deeds of Empire, 1979

IN ORDER to think seriously about empire as a way of life, we must first choose a strategy of inquiry that is appropriate to the subject. Then we must define the basic terms involved, and outline the process whereby the different elements of society are integrated into an overall outlook and culture.

I

Let us begin with the concept, way of life. There are many ways to define this seemingly soft and fuzzy but nevertheless very tangible aspect of human existence. All cultures have recognized the reality of the phenomenon, and many people—philosophers as well as sociologists, economists as well as historians, and anthropologists as well as political theorists and students of literature—have offered descriptions and definitions. Drawing upon a good many such efforts, I want here to work with this proposition: a way of life is the combination of patterns of thought and action that, as it becomes habitual and institutionalized, defines the thrust and character of a culture and society.

In the classic German word, it is a *Weltanschauung*, a conception of the world and how it works, and a strategy for acting upon that outlook on a routine basis as well as in times of crisis. If you prefer an Anglo-Saxon formulation, consider it this way: each society holds in common certain assumptions about reality, and every day those assumptions guide and set limits upon its members—their awareness and perception, their understanding of cause and consequence, their sense of options, and their range of action.

"We stabilize around a set of concepts . . . and hold them dear," explains one sociologist. "At each moment of each day, we make the same mistakes . . . we consider that our own personal consciousness *is* the world." Or, in the words of a historian, "those unconsciously accepted presuppositions which, in any age, so largely determine what men think about the nature of the universe and what can and cannot happen in it."

In thinking about empire as a way of life, we must consider the dynamics of the process as well as a static description of the empire at any particular moment. The empire as a territory and as activities dominated economically, politically, and psychologically by a superior power is the *result* of empire as a way of life. This is particularly important in the case of the United States because from the beginning the persuasiveness of empire as a way of life effectively closed off other ways of dealing with the reality that Americans encountered.

It is next necessary to clarify the key terms *empire* (and *imperial*), *colonialism*, and *imperialism*. As with many words that deal with primary human actions, *empire* has been used to name several kinds of activity, relationships, policies, and institutions. Any extended discussion of such denotations and connotations inevitably becomes an exercise in splitting ever more hairs until the central issue is lost in the mangy debris. All that said, it is nevertheless true that empire has consistently been used to specify two associated, but nevertheless different, relationships.

One is the union of initially separate but physically and politically and socially related units of population under one central authority. The resort to force by one or more of those entities may or may not be a major element in the process, but in either case the result is an empire governed as an imperial system. The will, and power, of one element asserts its superiority. This meaning of empire is illustrated by the United Kingdom of England, Scotland, and Wales; and, as I will argue a bit later, by the government created by the Constitution over the original and significantly independent states of America.

The other meaning of empire concerns the forcible subjugation of formerly independent peoples by a wholly external power, and their subsequent rule by the imperial metropolis. One thinks here of the First Americans and of the northern half of Mexico seized by conquest in the 1840s by the United States and integrated into its imperial system. Or of England's assault upon Ireland.

The term *colonialism* has been devalued by sloppy usage. Here again, therefore, we are wise to settle upon two basic meanings. The substance involves the large-scale transfer and subsequent rule of people from (or under the control of) the imperial metropolis to an area previously unoccupied, or populated by people who cannot resist the invasion and are therefore conquered or destroyed. Such examples include Great Britain colonizing North America (and Australia), and transferring and colonizing Africans to its southern regions— a system of slavery carried on by the United States after 1776.

The other meaning of colonialism is more complicated, and a case can be made for viewing it as a separate phenomenon that emerged during the transition from classic colonialism to imperialism. This kind of colonialism did involve, however, the shift of people from the metropolis to the sub-jugated area as a matter of official policy, and for that reason it seems more useful to consider it as a particular kind of colonialism.

Here the crucial element concerns the *function* of the people sent out from the metropolis. Rather than being charged to settle and populate the area, they were (and still are) dispatched to rule an indigenous society by setting limits on the choices the natives *can* consider. Thus the form is often called *administrative colonialism*. Consider here the British in India and Africa, and the United States in Cuba and the Philippines.

The term *imperialism* is even more thoroughly muddled and confused. The semantic trouble began with the casual appropriation of the word *imperial*, originally associated with empire, to describe an evolving set of *different* relationships between advanced industrial societies and the rest of the world. It was then frazzled and fuzzied by an English Liberal named John A. Hobson and a Russian revolutionary who chose to call himself Lenin, both of whom employed it to explain those relationships as well as to prophesy the future. All in all, the word disappeared into a swamp of analysis, propaganda, projection, and nonsense.

But the term *imperialism* does have an irreducible meaning: the loss of sovereignty—control—over essential issues and decisions by a largely agricultural society to an industrial metropolis. Superior economic power subjects an inferior political economy to its own preferences. Adam Smith said it once and for all: the city enjoys and exploits a structural advantage over the country. The metropolis routinely displays and occasionally uses its military power, and metropolitan advisers (official and private, academic and corporate) are always on guard as supervisory personnel, but the essence of imperialism lies in the metropolitan domination of the weaker economy (and its political and social superstructure) to ensure the

extraction of economic rewards. One thinks here of the relationship between Great Britain and Argentina between 1870
and 1914, between the United States and many countries in
the western hemisphere (Canada as well as Cuba and Panama), and between all industrial powers and what has become known as the Third World.

If we accept that basic definition of imperialism, then we
have no trouble dealing with similar relationships—superior
over inferior—between industrial societies. That is a more
complicated and fluctuating involvement, but it can and has
produced serious tension and widespread violence. Indeed,
the outbreak of World Wars I and II, as well as America's
relationship with Western Europe and Japan after 1945, can
be understood as manifestations of that variation on the
theme of modern imperialism.

II

Any world-view—from self-containment in the traditional
Chinese sense to the global expansionism of Western Europe
after the voyages of Columbus and Vasco da Gama in the
1490s—is defined by the way people integrate the basic elements of organized society. Those components are usefully
defined as the economic, the political, the social and intellectual, and the military. The importance assigned to those factors varies under different conditions, and is determined
through various processes.

The people who lived along the Pacific Northwest coast
before America was invaded by Europeans, for example, enjoyed a surplus of economic resources within a relatively
small geographic area; but the Aborigines of the Central Australian Desert wandered over millions of square miles in their
struggle to find enough water and food. Thus one culture
valued economic wealth as a means to acquire status by wasting the resources, while the other people accepted a subsis-

tence economy and stressed the importance of creating a community by honoring collective myths and rituals.

In a similar way, the hierarchy of values can develop through competition between the various elements or be guided by some general—inclusive—idea of the proper and most effective pattern of inter-relationships. The history of the United States offers an illuminating example of how those two methods or processes of integration can occur over time in one society. The Constitution was both the instrument and the symbol of a conscious decision to create a particular kind of system rather than to allow the society to develop through random competition between economic and other forces.

Once the Constitution was adopted, however, it created rules and defined the arena for competition between the various basic components of society: economic, political, social and intellectual, and military. Ideas did not become irrelevant, but they did become more narrowly related to one or another of those four fundamental areas of life. At the same time, economic objectives and activity (whether defined by individuals or groups) steadily took precedence over other aspects of life. Even so, each element vied with the others to determine what would be given priority at the local, state, regional, and national levels. In a fundamental sense, therefore, vigorous political action by people stressing one concern over others became the method of determining the hierarchy of values that defined the culture and its way of life.

That meant that The State became the instrument of integrating the parts into a whole. Not the state as Ohio or Alabama, but The State as the institution wherein priorities were decided and implemented as policy. As when the demand for more land changed domestic policy or produced a war. It is not surprising, therefore, that most of us think of The State as simply the government. And often, within that framework, and depending upon our particular concern, as one specific department or agency. When we are upset about foreign policy, for example, we tend to think of The State as the White House and the State Department connected by a tunnel known as the National Security Council. Note, and keep in mind, how we have abstracted specific people into capitalized, impersonal institutions.

Given time to think and reflect, we realize that the government or The State is really various groups of people. As far as foreign affairs are concerned, The State consists of the following such units. Elected officials and their appointed staffs; the national civil bureaucracies (such as Commerce, State, and Treasury) composed of appointed and hired personnel; the military (including the CIA); the civil police forces (especially the FBI); and the judicial system, including the community of lawyers.

It has recently become routine to think and talk about those people as The Establishment. The phrase has become a popular way of avoiding the harsh truths about power that are more directly and clearly expressed in the phrase The State, while at the same time recognizing that some people exercise more power than most people. Such fuzzing of reality further abstracts specific people as vague shapes haunting the corridors of power.

The man who revived the term The Establishment, Henry Fairlie, based his usage on a sophisticated understanding of why and how a way of life, a world-view or *Weltanschauung*, informs and guides the people who constitute The State. The Establishment, he insightfully insists, "is not those people who hold and exercise power as such. It is the people who create and sustain the climate of assumption and opinion within which power is exercised by those who do hold it by election or appointment." He is making a crucial distinction.

The people defined by Fairlie do get elected or appointed to high and influential positions. That is because they are recognized as makers of the way of life, but also because they are powerful as leaders in the economic, intellectual, and other areas of society. That does not subvert Fairlie's basic point. Those people are primarily important because they are, in or out of government, the human beings who order the priorities and relationships in terms of a system. They integrate the parts into a whole.

Thus we make a serious mistake if we confuse The Establishment with The State. For in doing that we remove ourselves from any consequential part in shaping our way of life. In the first place, we foster an illusion that electing or appointing different people will produce or lead to a change in the outlook or *Weltanschauung*. But we are in reality changing the wrong people, and the recent rise in political and electoral apathy indicates a rudimentary awareness of that truth.

Second, and in a more fundamental sense, that mistake removes us from the consequential debate about shaping our way of life. The central issue here does not involve the small, or elitist nature of The Establishment: all groups of people produce leaders who become spokesmen of the shared interest or idea. The important consideration is our lack of participation in the dialogue. In a republic or a democracy, we the citizens are supposed to order the priorities and relationships between the economic, the political, the social and intellectual, and the military aspects of life through an on-going discussion. *We are supposed to be The Establishment*. As it is, we limit ourselves to choosing between generally minor variations on one theme composed by others.

It can be (and is) argued (or hoped) that the many divisions of labor within our advanced capitalist political economy guarantees that no Establishment can in practice define basic priorities or policies over any significant period of time. That is a serious proposition advanced by thoughtful people, and it cannot be dismissed out of hand. For that matter, the evidence from one era of American capitalism (roughly 1815 to 1896) provides substance for that proposition. There was extensive and vigorous competition within and between the various elements of American society.

When applied to other periods, however, that pluralistic interpretation becomes less persuasive. If we concentrate on the years after 1896, for example, it becomes clear that competition reduced the number of competing units. All major segments of the economy came to be dominated by a tiny number of giant firms which shared an interest in controlling any new rivals, and establishing rules and procedures to control their part of the marketplace.

Technological innovations created new industries, to be sure, but the process of consolidation and concentration was also accelerated. The automobile industry, for example, soon became the preserve of a handful of huge corporations (the largest of which was intimately tied to the biggest chemical firm). So, too, with food processing and merchandising (and the fertilizer industry), oil and related products, and even contemporary products like television sets and other electronic items, computers, and the gathering and marketing of information.

Every such segment of the economy ultimately produced leaders in the idiom and style of J. P. Morgan, the first national giant of the 20th-century banking and financial community. He recognized and acted upon three fundamental truths of the new corporate political economy: 1. the so-called free marketplace was not a random collection of entrepreneurs but rather a *system* of capitalists that could only be understood as a *system;* 2. that the system was plagued by inherent and serious structural problems; and hence 3. the elements in the marketplace must be ordered and coordinated to sustain the system.

Many key leaders supported Morgan's analysis, and the subsequent actions to regulate, balance, and rationalize the

American political economy were nothing less than an effort by the private giants and the government to plan or program the operation of the political economy. Sometimes the two groups labored together, other times separately or even as adversaries; and, especially during the early decades of the 20th century, the citizenry participated actively in the process. But the history of that dynamic interaction, and particularly the story of how the citizens were increasingly limited to choosing between policies formulated by the corporations or the government (or the two in collaboration), makes it apparent that all those protagonists accepted an imperial way of life.

Hence it is clear, despite the ever increasing power of an ever smaller minority of people "who create and sustain the climate of assumption and opinion," that the citizenry was involved in the development, consolidation, and entrenchment of one particular outlook. Very simply, Americans of the 20th century liked empire for the same reasons their ancestors had favored it in the 18th and 19th centuries. It provided them with renewable opportunities, wealth, and other benefits and satisfactions including a psychological sense of well-being and power.

But the costs and dangers of that imperial way of life have in our lifetimes become ever greater and more obvious. At the same time, by transforming the people who comprise both The Establishment and The State into abstract functionaries within the institutions which we revere as the symbols and agencies of our government, we have subverted the basic American axiom that we the citizens are supposed to formulate our outlook and our way of life.

In that fundamental sense, the cost of empire is not properly tabulated in the dead and maimed, or in the wasted resources, but rather in the loss of our vitality as citizens. We have increasingly ceased to participate in the process of self-government. We have become ever more frustrated and fatalistic, and hence concerned with individual gratification. Finally, we deny any responsibility; and, as part of that ultimate abdiction of our birthright, indignantly deny that the United States is or ever was an empire.

But that is to deny our own history. We have transformed our imperial way of life from a culture that we built and benefited from into an abstract self-evident Law of Nature that we must now re-examine in light of its costs and consequences. It is, we shrug, simply the way of the world. Empire is freedom. Empire is liberty. Empire is security.

We may well be doomed by our acceptance of the imperial dogma that democracy is dependent upon a surplus of space and resources. Our only chance is to talk straight to ourselves and not flinch. During the Cuban Missile Crisis of 1962, Secretary of State Dean Rusk proudly and a bit self-righteously used that idiom in praise of empire. "We stood eyeball to eyeball and the other fellow blinked."

This time it is ourselves we must look in the eye—and neither blink nor turn away. Let us confront our imperial way of life.

CHAPTER ONE
Born and Bred of Empire

Riches do not consist in having more Gold and Silver, but in having more in proportion than the rest of the World, or than our Neighbours, whereby we are enabled to procure to ourselves a greater Plenty of the Conveniences of Life than comes within the reach of Neighbouring Kingdoms and States.

JOHN LOCKE, 1691

THE 19th- and 20th-century empire known as the United States of America began as a gleam in the eyes of various 16th-century critics of, and advisers to, Elizabeth I; and not improbably as a thought in Her Majesty's own mind. In the language of our time, England was then a backward and underdeveloped small island: poor, weak, and constantly torn by internal social conflict. Many other countries dismissed it as a pathetic excuse for a nation and raided its commerce with impunity. The frontier of Rome had become a leftover enclave.

Looking out upon the world in 1550, even the most unimaginative Englishman could see that the Portuguese, the Spanish, and the French—even the Dutch—were exploring and expropriating much of the newly discovered world. The English faced a choice: they could concentrate their resources, energy, and will to organize and develop themselves as a small but dynamic and creative community, or they could galvanize themselves to join the scramble for the globe.

It was not a hypothetical choice. Throughout human history various peoples have resisted the temptations of empire. One thinks here, for example, of the Japanese during many centuries of their development; or of the Chinese deciding to break up and burn the great fleets of Admiral Cheng-Hô that had reached the east coast of Africa long before the Portuguese. For that matter, some British and American imperial spokesmen have been candid enough to acknowledge the virtues of the other option. A smaller, non-imperial society enjoys not inconsiderable rewards. "Human problems can be truly perceived which in larger social structures must more or less necessarily be sacrificed. . . . People were conscious of what can be named serenity or dignity of human nature."

Thus empire as a way of life was never, even in the beginning, the only alternative open to us as Americans. Indeed, various minorities (and occasionally pluralities) amongst us have from time to time argued and agitated for a non-imperial outlook. And a significant number of those who chose the imperial option, such as James Madison, were excruciatingly aware that they were challenging an older, awesome wisdom. But the historian must record that America was born and bred of the British Empire.

I

The difficult labor of creating that empire occupied the English for many generations, and in the beginning they struggled primarily to impose order upon their own island. It was a painful process that involved asserting London's power over Scotland and Wales, *the creation of an empire within the island*, and the development of a dynamic economy. None of it was easy, and Britain remained divided, poor, weak, and backward well into the 16th century. The economic progress that did occur—as in textiles—was uncoordinated and characterized by serious and costly fluctuations, and agriculture was chronically sick. A boom in the wool trade from 1550 to 1552, for example, shortly collapsed and the society once again faced economic stagnation and social violence.

Over the years, various monarchs had tried to promote economic growth and social stability by decrees and laws designed to encourage, direct, and integrate the system. Thus Edward I (r. 1272–1307) terminated some foreign enterprises and focused the wool trade on exports to Antwerp; and Edward III extended those efforts as he dealt with domestic unrest and waged a long (1333–60) war with France. The Ordinance of Labourers and the Statute of Labourers were attempts to control wages and prices in an equitable relationship, for example, as well as measures to put every man to work and thereby help agriculture. And Richard II's Navigation Act of 1381 favored British traders and shippers against their foreign competitors. The profits of commerce were viewed as capital for domestic improvement.

Such fitful, even fumbling, efforts to build a system were refined, extended, and integrated by Elizabeth I and her successors. In its most general meaning, the term *system* bespeaks the arrangement of things to form a whole. Thus the various organs of the body constitute a system once their inter-relationships are understood. But here, and elsewhere in this essay, the word, and concept, *system* is also used to describe an attitude of mind. One is reluctant to interrupt Elizabeth's dramatically discreet visit to the London docks to knight Francis Drake as a cost-effective pirate who hijacked and brought home large amounts of Spanish gold; but we do need to comprehend her outlook and her purpose.

Psychologists and other students of human behavior have demonstrated that most people concentrate their attention, even vision, on one or a few of the elements that are parts of a whole. This is nicely demonstrated, for example, in the lack of composition in most people's snapshots. Their awareness of interrelationships is limited. This is particularly true when they confront a complex subject like society or culture. In a similar (and related) way, such people are inclined to think about society in terms of random action and chance.

Another group of people, however, do see the whole, and do conceptualize and think in terms of multiple inter-relations and a system. Queen Elizabeth I and her senior advisers, and others who later exercised power, were such people. They were not content to rely on the *chance* that random, uncoordinated activity by individuals or groups would produce the general welfare. Their philosophical resistance to that idea was reinforced by their knowledge of English history and their contemporary pragmatic experience. They simply could not take seriously the proposition that random activity somehow produced a coherent, consequential result. Most of them believed in God, or Some Power Out There, but they did not think it likely that He—or It—had either the time or the inclination to save fools who did not look after themselves. They did not share the belief, later to be so popular, that some Hidden Hand would coordinate random and self-interested activity to produce the common good. They sought instead to coordinate—*even to plan*—their efforts to realize their desired goals. They were in truth concerned to create a system through a conscious effort to integrate disparate elements into a purposeful pattern. They did not deny the reality of chance and random activity, but sought instead to absorb them within their purpose.

Such coordination can occur in two principal ways. The government asserts its will in an attempt to define and enforce various relationships designed to realize a program. Or private individuals and groups join hands—openly or covertly—to accomplish their objectives. As we shall see, both kinds of system building have been an integral part of American history. But here let us observe the efforts by Elizabeth I and others to create an imperial system.

Those who followed her in that labor were more knowledgeable about the intricacies of such an effort, but she exuded imperial verve and style. She encouraged and rewarded the dashing forays by Drake and others against the Spanish and the French. And she knew that when she touched the sword to Drake's shoulder that she was honoring a hero of a nasty business. Take from them to honor us and I will honor you. An honest and forceful imperial leader.

Karl Marx later cut through the romance of such activity and described it bluntly for what it was. To knight a pirate, he explained, is to legitimatize the primitive accumulation of the wealth that is essential to generate capitalist growth in a poor society. Small wonder, as one observer noted during Drake's heyday, that Mercury was christened the English "God of trade and theft." But such entrepreneurs had to be controlled, as well as encouraged, if the system was to create the general welfare. That was not only desirable in the social and moral sense, it was also necessary to prevent the imbalances that generated unrest or revolution.

"It stands not with the policy of the State," Sir Francis Bacon warned as early as 1601, "that the wealth of the Kingdom should be engrossed into a few graziers' hands." For in that case, Sir Edward Sandys explained, "the rich will eat out the poor." As a result, English leaders gradually created a pattern of legislation and other regulations that was designed to control the giants of the marketplace, improve the position of agriculture, and in general maintain balance and equity in the domestic side of the political economy.

But all those efforts were predicated upon imperial expansion. That was the engine of the system. No one stated the principle more candidly than Bacon. "The rebellions of the belly are the worst. The first remedy or prevention, is to remove, by all means possible that material cause of sedition, which is want and poverty in the estate. To which purpose serveth the opening and well balancing of trade; the cherishing of manufacturers; the banishing of idleness. . . . The increase of any estate must be upon the foreigner, for whatsoever is somewhere gotten is somewhere lost." William

Lane added a pithy amplification: the point of such expansion was "we to lyve off them and they not off us."

II

That imperial outlook and strategy were not seriously challenged by the coalition of interests and classes which between 1640 and 1649 made the English Revolution and created a republican Commonwealth led by Oliver Cromwell. It is conceivable, but highly improbable, that if the Levellers and other radicals within the revolutionary movement had won control of the country they would have freed the American colonies, ended other imperial ventures, and settled down to cultivate their domestic commonwealth. Not only were they children of the imperial way of life, but they were also vigorous evangelists of *their* particular truths. And, as the United States was to demonstrate, there is neither a logical nor a pragmatic connection between more freedom at home and less empire abroad.

As for Cromwell, he was a crusader and an imperialist. He assaulted his fellow-Protestant Dutchmen, as well as the Catholic Irish and Spanish, in the course of establishing the Rights of Free Englishmen. He was arrogantly confident that England's ideal constitution would claim "the patronage of the world." His judgment of other societies and cultures was classically imperial: they were "all sick." And his imperial legislation, such as the act forbidding the importation of goods except in English ships (or those of the nation producing the items), was explicitly designed to control world trade.

The English Revolution unquestionably strengthened the Rights of Free Englishmen and created a strong momentum toward more representative and responsible government. But it did not solve the problems of backwardness and underdevelopment, and hence British leaders continued and extended

their efforts to rationalize and expand a centrally directed imperial system. The resulting tension between freedom, order,
and prosperity created a paradox perhaps most strikingly
symbolized in the thought and career of John Locke.

Locke was at the center of English politics, both as an adviser to high officials and as a philosopher who evoked wide
public response, from 1660 to the end of the century. He is
important in the development of empire as a way of life not
because he was unique, but because he expressed the contra-
dictions of the imperial outlook with a special verve, clarity,
and style, and because he influenced large numbers of Americans.

Englishmen on both sides of the Atlantic responded to
him, for he expressed and clarified the basic elements of their
attitudes and thoughts: the concern with responsible, balanced (even limited) liberty; the assumption that progress
depended upon coordinated, even planned, action; and the
belief that—given the finite nature of the world—domestic
welfare and social peace required vigorous imperial expansion. "Riches do not consist in having more Gold and Silver,
but in having more in proportion than the rest of the World,
or than our Neighbours, whereby we are enabled to procure
to ourselves a greater Plenty of the Conveniences of Life than
comes within the reach of Neighbouring Kingdoms and
States."

Locke also provided a model for colonial Englishmen who
sought power in the name and exercise of freedom. In a
crucial sense, as historian Merle Curti pointed out many
years ago, Locke offered something to everybody. A yeo-
man, artisan, or mechanic could cite him in praise of liberty.
A merchant, squire, or politician could quote him on the
necessity of balance and order. And all of them shared his
concern with expansion.

Locke and other post-revolutionary leaders moved
vigorously to enlarge and integrate the American colonies as

an essential part of the empire. Their objective was to create a system ruled with a combination of firmness and permissiveness that honored the principles of an imperial commonwealth. There was never any question about London setting basic policy, or ensuring the English metropolis a favorable balance of trade (and allocation of resources). But the colonies were granted a significant degree of local autonomy, were protected militarily, and were granted economic favors (and opportunities) that guaranteed consequential profits and growth.

It is very easy to document the lack of perfection in the reality of the evolving empire. There were significant inequalities within the colonies, and in England; as well as a growing discrepancy in the pace and balance of development between the colonies and the British metropolis. Even so, the imperial way of life provided important gains for increasing numbers of Englishmen. And in the larger sense the most significant aspect of the empire was the success in transforming the American colonies from tiny, insecure outposts into dynamic societies generating their own progress. Whatever its costs, both then and later, the empire functioned effectively during the century after the English Revolution.

On the one hand, the American colonies prospered as part of the British Empire, and their developing strength, self-consciousness, and confidence were essential in moving them to *think* of revolution and in translating that idea into action. On the other hand, the successes of the Empire produced vast changes within Great Britain which led to the confrontation with the colonies. That dialectical process provides a classic example not only of the nature of change, but of the interaction between economic activity and political, intellectual, and social developments. It also produced another culture based on the proposition that expansion was the key to freedom, prosperity, and social peace.

CHAPTER TWO

A Psychologically Justifying and Economically Profitable Fairy Tale: The Myth of Empty Continents Dotted Here and There with the Mud Huts, the Lean-tos, and the Tepees of Unruly Children Playing at Culture

Conquer, occupy and possess. . . . [Acquire] dominion, title, and jurisdiction.

HENRY VII to JOHN CABOT, 1496

Happily there was a saving precedent: the Crusades had well established the principle that war conducted in the interests of Holy Church was automatically just.

FRANCIS JENNINGS, *The Invasion of America*, 1975

LOCKE SAID it as well as anyone and more honestly than most: empire as a way of life involves taking wealth and freedom away from others to provide for your own welfare, pleasure, and power. Even so, others like Henry VII were respectably candid. Elizabeth I may have been discreet in knighting Drake, but her general directive was straight to the point: conquer any "remote heathen and barbarous lands" and impose proper government upon such savages. And in 1607 the directors of the Virginia Company of London were properly blunt. Knowing the purpose of settlement, they warned their colonists that "you cannot carry yourselves so toward them [the First Americans] but they will grow discontented with your habitation."

In the broader sense, however, the English and other European empire builders developed a contradictory and convoluted (if at times sophisticated) argument that justified their imperial activities in India, Africa, Asia, and America. That elaborate ideology was not simply or only a callous or cynical rationalization. Whatever their roots in the mundane realities of greed, such overarching systems of ideas take on a life of their own and function (and become accepted) as engines of action.

Thus it is revealing and useful to explore them on their own terms. My emphasis here is on the English confrontation with the established seaboard, but it applies with equal force to the subsequent enslavement of Africans and the destruction of the First Americans west of the Appalachian Mountains. Both were the motifs of the imperial coin.

Karl Marx once remarked, in a phrase that illuminates his exasperated outburst that he was not a Marxist, that the past weighs like an Alp upon the brain of the living. Old ideas influence a new reality. One could have great fun, and perhaps make a contribution to wisdom, by arguing that therein lies the genesis of psychoanalysis. But let us here use Marx's insight as a guide to exploring the origins and character of the imperial characterization of its victims. How we perceive our victims tells us much indeed about ourselves. Such overarching ideologies are inherently complicated, giving rise to different emphases and interpretations among historians, sociologists, anthropologists, political theorists, and ethnohistorians. We can properly begin, therefore, by outlining two of those arguments.

The problem confronting the English (and other European) empire builders was very simple. Even by their own rules, the unilateral, uninvited, and unprovoked intrusion over thousands of miles by one culture into the life and affairs of another could not be explained or justified by an appeal to self-defense. That primal right could plausibly be invoked, even at best, *only after the initial penetration had occurred and was resisted*. Hence the initial invasion must be justified by some other logic. Over the years, scholars dealing with that problem have tended to separate into two groups: one emphasizes the importance of color (blacks and browns are inferior); the other stresses Christianity (heathens are agents of the Devil and so must be converted or destroyed).

ruth those explanations are less contradictory or
han mutually supportive and reinforcing of empire
of life. Whatever its origins in the eastern Mediter-
ran , Christianity became a European phenomenon and,
despite the brownish hue of some Mediterranean Catholics
and Orthodox believers, they were generally lighter—
"whiter" than the uninformed or unpersuaded in India, Asia,
Africa, and America. Heathens were on sight generally
darker than converts, and hence visually tainted by the domestic force of the Devil who was always presented as black.

That evidence, such as it was, was reinforced by other
kinds of proof. Europeans were highly conscious—one might
even say hypersensitive—of having come through an extremely difficult and perilous time of troubles. Not only had
they been challenged by Islamic and other non-believers, but
the infidels had probed close to the vitals of their own way of
life. They had also been tested in horrendous trials by dis-
ease and other disasters. But they *had* survived. It was more
than a bit like death and resurrection. Given their Christianity, that was understandably interpreted as a sign of the
Grace of God. Their disputations and wars with each other
about the nature of the true faith were tactical not strategic:
not about the faith, but only about how best to interpret and
extend it.

Thus it is important to realize that Jennings's perceptive
remark about the Holy Church has to do with secular as well
as religious ideology. It was not only that Christianity was
the true religion. The faithful had survived and were moving
toward the assertion of their superiority. They had developed better ships and more deadly weapons to subdue the
Eastern infidels. They had triumphed over pestilence and
poverty to build cities. They had controlled dissidence
through the creation of centralized instruments of government. And they had organized economic activity well
enough to generate a growing surplus (well, at least for
some).

To employ the science and the language of a later century, there was a non-articulated social Darwinism in all of that: a preview of the sense, if not the theory, of the superiority inherent in mere survival and continuation. It was not formulated in those terms, or with those footnotes, but it was nevertheless a very real and present and powerful element of the developing imperial way of life. There was, in short a secular Holy Church with its own doctrine of superiority.

Those complementary dogmas, sacred and secular, did not immediately or inevitably produce a hard-line racist outlook. There emerged instead a spectrum of attitudes, among both religious and lay thinkers, that can usefully be described in terms of two contradictory images: the Noble Savage and the Ignoble Savage. The former, a combination of romanticism and superciliousness, developed as the faith and idiom of the more humane group of English and American imperialists. They considered themselves superior, and justified the imposition of imperial power on that basis, but they modified such arrogance in several respects.

To begin with, they acknowledged that some aspects of "savage" life were worth serious consideration and perhaps even emulation. They were impressed, for example, by the significantly (even statistically) lower incidence of violence within First American societies, and by the limits generally imposed by those cultures upon inter-societal warfare. They responded favorably—or at least thoughtfully and tolerantly —to the more relaxed attitudes about sex, marriage, and divorce, and to the different idioms of personal hygiene (as in daily bathing) and medical treatment. And they recognized, however cautiously, that the religion of the First Americans—including its emphasis on dreams—bespoke a sense of awe and wonder that was related to their own belief in spirits and miracles.

Those more relaxed or benevolent imperialists also acknowledged the impressive skills of the First Americans. Not only were they good farmers (who cleared enough land to let

half lie fallow), but they demonstrated a sophisticated understanding of how to create and sustain a symbiotic relationship with the land. They did not graze cattle or pigs, to
be sure, but they did create pasture for deer. They also
displayed an ability to organize a division of labor, both
within and between cultures, that led to a remarkable system
of trade over long distances that involved food, metals, and
other commodities.

For all those reasons, the group of English people (and
later Americans) that we can usefully call the soft imperialists—religious and secular—did not become racists. They
were arrogant, supercilious, and patronizing, but they did
separate themselves from the racists on three vital issues.
First, they considered the First Americans human. Second,
they acknowledged their achievements. And, third, on those
grounds, they considered it possible and desirable to elevate
the Noble Savage into at least partial civilization. They left
the future open.

It would be pleasant, and surely uplifting, to report that
such soft imperialists carried the day. They did not. Indeed
not. But even so the soft imperialists were and remained important. If nothing else, they now and again prevented the
hard-line imperialists from plunging joyfully into disaster.
American historians, along with their fellow intellectuals,
display their imperial temperament by cataloging people according to two categories: imperialists and anti-imperialists.
It is a less than helpful filing system. We Americans, let
alone our English forefathers, have produced very, very few
anti-imperialists. Our idiom has been empire, and so the
primary division was and remains between the soft and the
hard.

It all comes down to the question of whether one conquers
to transform the heathen into lower-class members of the empire or simply works them to death for the benefit of the imperial metropolis. Even if the softies win, empire is still the
way of life.

But the truth of it is that the hard-liners won. And so in that sense, at any rate, the question of racism is secondary. The primary question has always been the control of wealth and the liberty for some to do as they choose. Racism, the product of the image of the Ignoble Savage, began and survived as the psychologically justifying and economically profitable fairy tale. It provided the gloss for the harsh truth that empire, soft or hard, is the child of an inability or an unwillingness to live within one's own means.* Empire as a way of life is predicated upon having more than one needs.

Think of it this way: the English-American empire builders went first for the land cleared and cultivated by the First Americans. It was simply too much hard work to chop those trees and root those stumps. Easier by far to take the land already cleared by the heathens. And take their food to survive. We have all heard, as children of children of children, how our ancestors in Virginia and Massachusetts were saved by the surplus produce from the gardens cultivated by those Ignoble Savages. And it is true. Hence it cannot be true that they were nomads who misused the land. John Winthrop of Massachusetts, churchman though he was, was simply wrong—if not worse—when he said that the First Americans "inclose noe land neither have any settled habitation." They treasured and cherished all the land they shared in common.

But, good Christian imperial lawyer that he was, Winthrop was making the best case for grabbing the land. After all, as Cromwell had said, all others were "sick." And you were sick if you did not sit on it all the time. No fences and no cattle meant "noe other but a naturall right to those countries." Hence, "if we leave them sufficient for their use we may lawfully take the rest." The "rest" meant wherever

---

* As Edmund S. Morgan has demonstrated in *American Slavery, American Freedom: The Ordeal of Colonial Virginia*, racism also came to be used as an instrument to control the domestic tension that was caused by the uneven distribution of the wealth acquired through imperial policies.

they were not located at any given moment, and the law was imperial fiat. Winthrop was a soft imperialist in that he hoped to convert the heathen to embrace their doom, but a hard imperialist in acquiring the loot.

There and elsewhere empire was ruthless. Even so, all such beliefs and rationalizations which prompted and sanctified numerous imperial wars killed fewer First Americans than the diseases imported by the European invaders. The gunfire removed the hardy. Prior to the appearance of the Europeans there were probably between 10 and 12 million people living north of the Rio Grande River. And it seems very likely, given the existence of surplus-producing agriculture, that the population was increasing on a regular basis.

Then came the first Spanish and French, followed by the fleets of fishermen to the north and the early colonies that failed to survive. The coughs, the sneezes, and the laying on of hands were like the bombs over Hiroshima and Nagasaki. The instruments of mass death by smallpox and other diseases. By the time of Jamestown and Plymouth, as Jennings observes, the "American land was more like a widow than a virgin."

Then the soft imperialists subverted their grand ideal. For it was impossible to preserve the Noble Savage and at the same time bring him into the imperial world. The consolidation of English settlements generated extremely powerful non-military forces of destruction. We are perhaps too preoccupied with the role of violence in imperial expansion. Having experienced violence, I do not discount its power or persuasion; or, in other respects, its convenience in the matter of conquest. It is difficult, for example, to discount the urge to mayhem generated by the discovery that tobacco earned significant profits. After all, no superior persons would weary themselves by clearing the brush and forests when rifles would drive the First Americans from land already prepared.

All that said, the disruption of First American cultures caused by ostensibly mundane and innocent economic

exchange, let alone the fur industry, was a
cutting devastating swathes through a c
tegrated way of life. As it was with smallpox, so
trade. Imperial philosophers are very serious abou
merce for sound reasons: it subverts an established way
life and creates a dependency upon the metropolis. Trade between unequals is as harmless as a magnet around a compass.

The commerce in guns, knives, other tools, and blankets
quickly altered preferences and destroyed indigenous skills
among the First Americans. Even without the almost incalculable effect of huge amounts of alcohol (a major if neglected industry in all imperial expansion), that dependency
was a progressively demoralizing force. And the fur trade
was far more complex than the term *trade* indicates. It substi-
tuted commercial hunting for balanced cropping of the har-
vest and thus subverted the supply of food and clothing. It
imposed upon the women an assembly-line system of preparing the pelts that disrupted family and tribal life, and it
created a preview of the share-cropping system that later
kept black Americans hostage to the imperial way of life even
after they were ostensibly free.

As with the Africans who were colonized in the British-
American empire as slaves, the First Americans made enormous contributions to the way of life developed by their con-
querors. Their concern and generosity ensured the survival
of the first English settlements. They taught the invaders
how to explore and sustain themselves in the far reaches of
the continent. And they had developed at least half of the
crops that provided the imperial Americans with their sustenance. Indeed, they taught the Europeans how to be pioneers.

And for that they were destroyed. In the beginning as pos-
sessors of cultivated land and as pawns in the wars of empire
between European powers, and ultimately as disposable
commodities by erstwhile colonials expanding their own empire.

CHAPTER THREE

A Revolution for Self-Government and Empire

Some fitter day shall crown us the Masters of the Main,
In giving laws and freedom to subject France and Spain,
And all the isles o'er Ocean shall tremble and obey
The Lords, the Lords, the Lords of North America.

Poem in the *Virginia Gazette*, 1774

This form of government [The Constitution], in order to effect its pur-
poses, must operate not within a small but an extensive sphere.

JAMES MADISON to THOMAS JEFFERSON, 1787

[Our success] furnishes a new proof of the falsehood of Montesquieu's
doctrine, that a republic can be preserved only in a small territory.
The reverse is the truth.

THOMAS JEFFERSON, Inaugural Address, 1801

THE BRITISH triumph over the French in the long war from 1754 to 1763, which delivered Canada into their hands, posed a tricky problem for the victors. The State needed money. The economic giants at home demanded ever more freedom and profit for themselves by limiting the freedom of the American colonies. And yet the Americans were becoming strong enough—and self-conscious enough—to resist the measures that would satisfy the Crown and the metropolitan behemoths.

If we step back from the bones and dust and blood of the cockpit of daily politics, we can see that the British mercantilists were reaping the troubles of their successes. There is no question that empire provides benefits for a few of the people all of the time, and even for all of the people some of the time—including various groups in the colonies. The difficulty arises when the powers-that-be in the metropolis insist upon economic or political policies that antagonize or threaten the elite in the provinces. For that enables the element within the upper class that wants independence to lead (and manipulate) the masses. They can thus isolate or overpower those members of their class who are reluctant to break the umbilical cord that has provided ideological, political, and social security—and economic sustenance.

Think only of Joseph Galloway of Pennsylvania and Samuel Adams of Massachusetts. Galloway was a thoughtful member of the elite who wanted to temporize: compromise contemporary differences, grow stronger, and bank the profits and the power of the natural course of events. Adams, an anti-colonial politician with a master's degree from Harvard, urged action before the imperial metropolis asserted ever stronger controls over the American political economy. He was hot for revolution in the name of liberty and the conquest of Canada.

We can begin to unravel the Adams paradox by examining the wisdom of Benjamin Franklin. His perceptive essay "Observations Concerning the Increase of Mankind, Peopling of Continents, etc." (1751) was perhaps the first integrated secular argument by a colonial that linked expansion with prosperity, social peace, and freedom. Given the propensity of people to procreate, he wrote, surplus land was essential to generate sustenance and wealth through agriculture and commerce. Furthermore, a crowded country became socially and politically corrupt and unstable. Thus there were two possibilities: North America, including Canada, could divide into several nations; or it could develop as the metropolis of a vastly more powerful British Empire.

When he wrote that analysis, and for many years thereafter, Franklin favored the second course of action. Compromise, woo the British, and become the metropolis. And, not surprisingly, he cast himself for a major role as one of the people who would be "properly called *Fathers*" of that grand empire. Along with those like Galloway, Franklin labored long hours to persuade his fellow colonists, and leaders in London, to accept his strategy. During the Albany Conference in 1754, for example, he proposed a coalition between the elites in London and America to handle the problems of expansion (Indians, taxes, armies, and the like) on a partnership basis; and he pushed the essentials of his plan, such as joint economic development, down to the eve of the revolution. But the British feared that such a policy would lead to the loss of control and profits, and Americans increasingly asserted their own claims to their own empire.

Near the end of the ensuing confrontation, Franklin adroitly presented himself as an advocate of independence and joined Sam Adams in agitating for the conquest of Canada—and added his own arguments for taking the Floridas and the West Indies. It was not so much that Adams and his street politics had proved superior to Franklin's theory as it was that the British failed to see the power of Franklin's argument that they could continue to rule indefinitely by moving London to the Ohio River Valley. One cannot resist wondering whether Franklin enjoyed a chuckle when, centuries later, the London Bridge was sold to a private real-estate developer in Arizona.

Adams and Franklin are less to be understood as adversaries than as powerful protagonists of the different elements that created the American version of empire as a way of life. For, despite all his denial of upper-class ties, his plotting in the back room of his favorite inn in Boston, and his militant rhetoric about liberty, Adams was a man who honored and sustained the Puritan tradition of *ordered* freedom. Like many later Americans who thought of themselves as radicals (even liberals), Adams was a crusader who wanted to save his fellow citizens in the course of reforming the world and creating an empire.

If we consider the mix of religion, natural rights philosophy, capitalist political economy, and cultural superiority, then Adams is properly honored as a symbol as well as an organizing genius of the emerging American empire. He was a master of arousing, coordinating, focusing, and energizing those attitudes, beliefs, and ambitions into a political movement. And he knew how to pick effective associates, like Joseph Warren, and give them a loose rein. If he was not the father of the Revolution, he was surely the midwife.

But Adams did not, probably could not, synthesize all those ideas into an imperial philosophy. That was very largely the labor of two Virginians, Thomas Jefferson and James Madison. The point here is not elitist: those two dear friends and neighbors of the slave-owning aristocracy did not invent and then impose an imperial way of life upon their fellow Americans. After all, Daniel Boone and his unremembered but no less adventurous allies were the facts behind the ideas. Jefferson and Madison simply put it all together in a way that excited true believers and persuaded doubters.

We need to begin, therefore, with the bricks with which they built the imperial foundation. Winthrop's faith in America as a City on the Hill and then as another Israel was echoed in the remark by Jonathan Edwards "that God might in [America] begin a new world in a spiritual respect." Edwards was in some ways highly skeptical of imperial ventures and tried to devise a working compromise with the First Americans, and hence his crusading hope is all the more revealing of the underlying attitudes. Other New Englanders stressed the secular Holy Church. James Otis, only slightly less important than Sam Adams, rhapsodized about "so glorious an empire."

And Warren put it this way: "I must indulge a hope that Britain's liberty, as well as ours, will eventually be preserved by the virtue of America." John Adams, who unlike his cousin Sam, flaunted his upper-class credentials, thought that the colonial era of America's history was only "the opening of a grand scheme and design in Providence for the illumination of the ignorant, and the emancipation of the slavish part of mankind all over the earth."

But southerners were not idle. Think only of Boone, arguing by example that the First Americans could—and should—

be replaced by noble white men. Or Richard Henry Lee demanding a navy to protect exports. And the poets. Perhaps especially the poets. Consider the anonymous author published in 1774 in the *Virginia Gazette:*

> Some fitter day shall crown us the Masters of the Main,
> In giving laws and freedom to subject France and Spain,
> And all the isles o'er Ocean shall tremble and obey
> The Lords, the Lords, the Lords of North America.

That bit of doggerel about "giving laws and freedom" is crucial to an understanding of the role of natural rights in the evolution of the American version of empire as a way of life. Many people have recognized the importance of that transformation of the specific Rights of Free Englishmen, rooted in communal experience, into an abstract, unlimited assertion of leadership of all humankind. Almost half a century ago, for example, historian and political scientist Arthur K. Weinberg said it this way: a "people believing itself a supreme contributer to the needs of all other peoples will conclude . . . that the rights essential to its existence or healthful development are weighted with the rights of all mankind."

In our own time, Yehoshua Arieli has, in his essay *Individualism and Nationalism in American Ideology*, marvelously illuminated Weinberg's insight. He makes it clear that Jefferson was the leader of the alchemists who transformed the Rights of Free Englishmen into the Right of Free Americans To Transform the World. Jefferson's letters, notes, and essays about "the people" transmuted a specific English heritage into what Arieli describes as abstract and timeless: "beyond the contingencies of history, and . . . identical with mankind." Jefferson was explicit. Americans had suffered and conquered not as members of the British community and body politic but only for themselves as the people. He reified the concrete into the ethereal and projected it into The Future.

We are back with Jennings and the secular Holy Church whose congregation is The World. America has meaning—or success—only as it realizes natural right and reason throughout the universe. As D. H. Lawrence phrased it, the "true myth of America" involves the dream of perpetual youth. There is no past, no present—only the Future. America "starts old, old, wrinkled and writhing in an old skin. And there is a gradual sloughing off of the old skin, towards a new youth." Or, as Crèvecoeur put it at the time of the Revolution, "the American is a new man."

Jefferson worked it out very neatly. "I strongly suggest that our geographical peculiarites may call for a different code of natural law to govern relations with other nations." But, quite in keeping with his lower-class bluntness, Thomas Paine said it all in twelve words. "We have it in our power to begin the world over again." Ben Franklin must have been proud, if a bit jealous, of his protégé's influence. Another bolt of lightning from another kite. But Jefferson had Madison, and it was Madison—rather than Paine or Franklin, or even Adams or Warren—who devised the way to begin the world over again.

II

Winning the Revolutionary War solved one problem but created many difficulties. Once free of the British, the American colonies slipped backward toward an earlier stage of capitalist development. To that extent, History *is* reversible, and we can learn by observing how different peoples deal with such situations. The colonies emerged victorious from their seven-year war, but they no longer enjoyed their preferential position within the empire (the vital West Indies trade, for example, was now closed to them), and they were divided, weak, and floundering without an integrated system. They were not as backward as England under Elizabeth I but they were certainly far less coherent and dynamic than they had been just prior to the battle for independence against the British metropolis.

None of that should surprise a modern observer who has watched the painful transition of China, Southeast Asia, India, and Africa from the imperial epoch into the age of independence. The disruption of an imperial system involves a process of disintegration that leaves the former colony alone in the world capitalist marketplace. Not in the metaphorical sense of *as if*, with the poets, but rather *as is*, with the hungry babies. Revolutionary success brings trouble as well as exhilaration, not enough food as well as moral and psychic strength, inferiority as well as potential bargaining power, and difficult decisions as well as freedom of choice.

As now, so then. Suddenly outside the British Empire, the thirteen free American states faced fundamental problems and clashing alternatives. Each could go its own way as a separate mercantilist system, join close neighbors in a largely independent regional federation, compromise to form a stronger confederation, or create a new imperial system. As the debate gathered momentum, each state began to legislate its own monetary system, navigation acts, and related mercantile measures. Southerners and New Englanders spoke candidly about separation into two governments. And others made unsuccessful efforts to infuse the government under the wartime Articles of Confederation with energy, purpose, and policy.

But northerners proved indifferent or openly antagonistic to the trans-Appalachian concern for obtaining commercial rights down the Mississippi and on through New Orleans to the markets of the world. Southern squires grew increasingly restive and apprehensive about being isolated and exploited as agricultural workers paying commercial and financial tribute to northern merchants—or having the western lands preempted by crude yeomen aspiring to plantation mansions. And many of those westerners fondled thoughts of their own empire.

Weak and troubled, many Americans increasingly turned back to their imperial heritage for a solution. As George Washington phrased it in 1783, perhaps more in hope than certainty, the not-so-united states were "a rising empire." Franklin had never changed his basic argument for expansion, and others like the Revolutionary leader Samuel Adams continued to argue the need for taking Canada. Southerners sought the Floridas and supported the western drive for the Mississippi and New Orleans. William Henry Drayton of South Carolina, a planter and politician of considerable importance, put it this way: "a new Empire, stiled the United States of America. . . . That bids fair, by the blessing of God, to be the most glorious of any upon Record." Still others stressed the need to move against the First Americans and the British in the Ohio Valley and Great Lakes region. And men of all sections grew ever more concerned about the need for a strong and effective trading and commercial policy in the world marketplace.

Those issues (and the related fears) prompted a group of leaders from the middle and southern states to gather in Annapolis, Maryland, to discuss the organization of a regional economic system. Instead, they quickly decided to create a new and far stronger national government. Under the leadership of Madison, the ensuing convention of 1787 in Philadelphia produced (behind locked doors) the Constitution. Both in the mind of Madison and in its nature, the Constitution was an instrument of imperial government at home and abroad.

While a student at Princeton, two of Madison's close friends were the poets Philip Freneau and Hugh Breckenridge. Individually and collectively, they composed countless verses: pornographic, sacrilegious, anti-Tory, and imperial. As for the latter, consider this gem of 1771 by Breckenridge and Freneau.

> Say, shall we ask what empires yet must arise, . . . and
> Where melancholy sits with eye forlorn
> And hopes for the day when British sons shall spread
> Dominion to the north and south and west
> From th' Atlantic thru Pacific shores.

Madison soon turned away from such undergraduate doggerel to the serious, extended study of economics and political theory. The post-Revolutionary crisis intensified that work and infused it with a sense of urgency. Had he been a philosopher king, it is clear that Madison would have given the country a classic mercantilist and imperial constitution with extensively centralized control over the political economy. As a practicing American politician, however, he faced several limitations. One was the power of state and regional feeling throughout the society. Even if he had not shared those ideals and emotions (though his involvement with some aspects of them was less extensive than that of other Americans), Madison would have had to compromise his ideal Constitution.

Finally, he faced a paradoxical kind of sentiment and psychology that seemed at first glance to be anti-imperial in nature. While most Americans actively wanted (and were trying to acquire, or actually taking) more land or trade, their experience with Great Britain between 1763 and 1783 left them skeptical or antagonistic toward a strong central government. Hence Madison had to persuade his compatriots to accept a system that exercised more control over them as well as other peoples. It was an extremely difficult problem, and thus Madison had to make an intellectual revolution before he could make an empire. He had, in short, to change people's minds—their way of thinking—about the relationship between empire and freedom.

As with many intellectual revolutions, Madison made his with ruthless simplicity. He simply turned conventional wisdom upside down, or inside out. The Revolutionary generation was impressively literate and knowledgeable about history and political theory (and literature); and the symbol of its understanding of the relationship between size, power, and freedom was based on Montesquieu's principle that liberty could exist only in a small state. Madison boldly argued the opposite: that empire was essential for freedom.

He explained it very clearly in a personal letter to Thomas Jefferson, an intimate friend he was most concerned to persuade to accept and support the new empire. "It may be said that the new Constitution is founded on different principles, and will have a different operation. I admit the difference to be material. . . . This form of government, in order to effect its purpose, must operate not within a small but an extensive sphere." The reason was simple. "Extend the sphere, and you take in a greater variety of parties and interests; you make it less probable that a majority of the whole will have a common motive to invade the rights of other citizens; or if such a common motive exists, it will be more difficult for all to feel it . . . to act in unison with each other."

Madison was nothing if not comprehensive. He was arguing that surplus social space and surplus resources were necessary to maintain economic welfare, social stability, freedom, and representative government. That was implicit in his related judgment that agrarian citizens were "the best basis of public liberty"; and explicit in his concern for a strong central government to acquire the land required for such people, and to protect and expand their export trade and to encourage their manufactures, shipping, and even fi-

nance. Not only was the Constitution grounded in an imperial logic, but it created a government armed with typically
mercantilist powers over the political economy.

The latter point has often been overlooked, largely because
of the different circumstances in which Madison operated,
and because mercantilist doctrine had become far more sophisticated by the 1780s than it had been during earlier centuries. But the Constitution's provisions concerning money
and finance, domestic and foreign commerce, foreign policy,
the President as commander in chief, and the control of un-
developed territories were in truth examples of classic mercantilist theory and practice.

Madison's contemporary critics missed none of those essential features of the Constitution. Robert Yates, for example, saw immediately that it would create an empire of the
existing states—an American version of the United Kingdom. Others, like "An Old Whig" and "A Federalist," who
offered their views in newspapers and pamphlets, recognized
the imperial nature of Madison's logic and prophesied the
biggest "consolidated empire" in history. "We are vain, like
other nations," another observer noted in sadness. "We wish
to make a noise in the world. . . . We are also, no doubt,
desirous of cutting a figure in History. Should we not reflect," he concluded, "[that] . . . extensive empire is a mis-
fortune to be depreciated."

Even so, most of the critics wanted the land and the markets—and the domestic stability—that the Constitution was
designed to provide through its imperial powers. As a result,
they were trapped in a wrenching predicament: accept the
Constitution or risk more social unrest (like Shays's Rebellion
in Massachusetts) and economic difficulties—or domination
by the more advanced political economy of Great Britain.
The "Old Whig," for example, understood the dilemma perfectly, but could do no more than plead for a slightly weaker

central government and explicit guarantees for the Natural Rights of Free Americans. Only a few like George Clinton of New York explicitly reasserted the validity of Montesquieu's thesis, but even he accepted the need to control domestic social unrest and admitted that the states would become an empire.

Perhaps the most revealing part of the story lies in the subsequent behavior of the critics. The overwhelming number rapidly embraced both the principles and the powers of the Constitution once they had lost the battle against adoption. Madison and his supporters had made their revolution: the logic and the instrument of empire had become the foundation of American society and the means to realizing the Future of liberty, freedom, opportunity, stability, and material welfare. Paraphrasing Washington's projection of hope into reality, Jedediah Morse asserted in 1789 that the erstwhile colonies "had risen into empire." He added that "it is well known that empire has been travelling from east to west. Probably her last and broadest seat will be America."

Thomas Hutchins, the geographer to the government, simply assumed that America would acquire the continent. That would enable the United States "to possess, in utmost security, the dominion of the sea throughout the world." That concern to create a maritime as well as a territorial empire also nibbled at the minds of Jefferson, Madison, and other southerners. Madison, for example, insisted as early as 1784 on the importance of controlling the coastline of the Gulf of Mexico. Jefferson (as well as Franklin) floated the idea that the eastern boundary of the United States was the far edge of the Gulf Stream. That argument presumably grew out of his new American system of natural rights: "the right to use a thing comprehends a right to the means necessary to its use." Jefferson would later carry that logic to its imperially absurd conclusion. In the meantime, the Kentucky Convention of 1788 reminded the new government of "the natural right of the inhabitants of this country to navigate the Mississippi."

Empire as a way of life steadily gathered momentum. Citing Jefferson's proposal to have the Great Seal of the United States depict the children of Israel being guided by a pillar of light, Weinberg concluded that "the doctrine of America's mission developed rather quickly into a dogma of special delegation."* Ezra Stiles, the president of Yale University, would probably have applauded Weinberg's analysis. Stiles was certain, as early as 1783, that the Good Lord would raise America "high above all nations which he has made." But perhaps it is said best of all in Federalist Paper No. XI. Let us "concur in erecting one great American system, superior to the control of all trans-Atlantic force or influence, and able to dictate the terms of the connection between the old and new world." Truly, a manifesto of empire as a way of life.

III

In one very important sense, History *is* the tale told by the winners. Those who have the power to ask the questions generally determine the answers. Others who struggle to turn the sword back upon the King (read The State or The Upper Class)—to say yes, *But*, or even *No*—usually lose. At least in the short run. All of which resolves the problem in a most practical way. For if you establish and sustain empire as a way of life for an indefinite period, then the critics die, become eccentrics to be humored, honored, and ignored, or damned as enemies of the truth. And the power.

But History also concerns itself with the *long* run: with what happens after even the winners are dead and rotting in

---

* A very similar interpretation of the final version of the Great Seal is provided by James A. Field, Jr., in *America and the Mediterranean World, 1776–1882.*

their finery. Yes, it does become very complicated. Particularly in America, where empire survived so many centuries. But eternity always, somehow, becomes tomorrow morning, and hence it is helpful to be armed with a truth from yesterday.

Paradox is the essence of History. In truth we will never *know*. But we can learn. So do not turn away when I suggest that a southern slave-owner made the best case against empire as a way of life. John Taylor of Caroline County, Virginia, was a man who originally thought that Madison and Jefferson would lead the country into the promised land of freedom and responsible government within community. But he watched and learned, and finally published an analysis that not only evoked a sense of doom within his own soul but provided the basis for all non-imperial philosophy.

Taylor was a trenchant and subtle thinker (if also a terribly convoluted writer—he was always making sure he was giving his opponent the worst of a questionable point). He began by accepting Madison's proposition that republican government could be extended over "spacious spheres." But he immediately introduced three vital reservations: the argument was true only if the society was "happily removed from real causes of collision with other nations"; only if expansion was organized as "a chain of republics"; and only if the central government was designed to favor man's good propensities over his evil tendencies.

But the Constitution, he warned, was an instrument of "energetic government," created and implemented through disingenuous procedures, and revealed an inherent dynamism which would create "*iron government*" and precisely such collisions with other nations. "The executive power of the United States is infected . . . with a degree of accumulation and permanence of power, sufficient to excite evil moral qualities." He noted, as examples, the President's power of patronage over the legislature and the courts, the inherent tendency toward secrecy, the treaty-making power. The resulting propensity to misuse the argument that all actions are justified by security requirements, and the direct and indirect power of the President to provoke or initiate a war.

Taylor constantly returned to the issue of foreign policy and war. "War," he pointed out, "is the keenest carving knife for cutting up nations into delicious morsels for parties and their leaders." And the Constitution did not provide any meaningful checks or controls over the executive's ability to decide the question: war is "unsubjected to publick opinion." He then noted that leaders in power identified themselves and their policies with national security, "and that therefore an opposition to the government, was an opposition to the nation itself." That "renders useless or impracticable the freedom of speech and of the press." The "only guarantees" against such subversion of the republic lay in local and regional conventions.

Adapted and augmented by other citizens over the years, Taylor's critique provided the basis for continuing opposition to empire as a way of life. But neither Taylor nor his successors ever generated the strength to overturn Madison's imperial *Weltanschauung*. The principal reasons for that failure are to be found in the raw power of imperial America to continue its expansion without suffering defeat in war, and in the ability of the resulting empire to provide benefits for a majority of the metropolitan populace.

Madison and most of his successors understood two subsidiary aspects of his system, and those insights enabled them, for many generations, to avoid most of the dangers inherent in their outlook. First, they recognized that the sphere (what a lovely euphemism—euphoria—for empire) could not be extended too far too fast because otherwise the empire could tumble out of control and disintegrate into separate regional communities that would become independent nations. Second, he sensed, along with many other south-

erners, the possibility of a visceral struggle over the nature of
the imperial political economy. The benefits of empire had to
be distributed on the basis of elementary equity in order to
prevent uncontrollable tensions between different interest
groups or classes or regions from erupting into social revolution. With one exception, the Civil War, Americans avoided
that pitfall.

Perhaps nothing dramatizes Madison's perceptiveness, and
the effectiveness of his heirs, than his prophecy. As an extremely sophisticated mercantilist who believed that the
world was finite, he recognized that someday there would be
no more surplus space or resources in the North American
continent. Near the end of his life he hazarded an informed
guess that such a situation would develop sometime near the
end of the 1920s, and forecast that the United States would
then turn toward some kind of monarchy.

If we recognize that Madison used *monarchy* as a word for
highly centralized and consolidated central government, we
can only marvel at his insight. For Franklin Delano Roosevelt and other leaders of the New Deal and subsequent ad-
ministrations did assert and acquire ever more power over
the political economy. As with their predecessors, however,
those neo-mercantilists of the mid- and late 20th century continued to be guided by an imperial *Weltanschauung*.

IV

The appeal and influence of Madison's rational argument for
imperial republicanism were steadily reinforced by individuals and groups who struggled to acquire ever more land and
trade, and by other ideas and emotions. One of the most
powerful of those forces was a belief from the past that was
gradually adapted to the new realities of America. For the
early religious sense of mission, so eloquently expressed in

Governor Winthrop's phrase—"wee shall bee as a City upon a Hill"—did not lose its power.

Many Americans, poor as well as powerful, and agricultural as well as urban, viewed themselves as agents of God's will and purpose. There is no reason, for example, to doubt the sincerity of John Quincy Adams of Massachusetts when he described the United States as "a nation, coextensive with the North American Continent, destined by God and nature to be the most populous and powerful people ever combined under one social compact."

As that example suggests, ordained missionaries were not the only people motivated (even driven) by that religious spirit to carry America's truth on across the Pacific to Asia, or back across the Atlantic to the Middle East. One cannot escape a strong sense, in this connection, that even though God has been pronounced dead in many different ways since the Reformation, He was still very much alive. One of the most sophisticated ways of transforming Him involved secularizing Him by equating Godliness with individual or collective success on earth. As one perceptive observer has noted, that meant that Christianity became increasingly "self-centered and ego-directed."

Thus the successful way becomes the Lord's way, and Everyman becomes a missionary of the American Dream in dealing with the Indians and others who are not following the American Way. If such people refuse to "open their minds to the idea of improvement," they are agents of the Devil who must be dealt with by force. Or, as phrased by Lewis Henry Morgan, the father of American anthropology, they must be educated to American conceptions of the "rights of property, and rights of citizenship, which are common to ourselves." Such examples, and they can be cited *ad infinitum*, remind one of Horace Walpole's caustic observation of 1762 that "every age has some ostentatious system to excuse the havoc it commits."

That comment serves to underscore the point that the secularization of God affected groups (and even an entire society) as well as individuals. If the person's sense of calling was transformed from honoring God's laws to prospering in the marketplace, then the nation's calling was changed from being a City on a Hill to being the active crusader to reform the world according to the American Dream.

That process, which continued throughout the 19th century, was greatly reinforced by the wholly secular idea that the American Revolution (including the conception and implementation of the Constitution) represented the perfect revolution. Americans came very quickly to view themselves as having discovered the ultimate solution to mankind's long search for the proper way to organize society. Jefferson encapsulated the outlook in his famous remark that America was "the world's best hope."

That belief had two imperial consequences. First, the behavior of other peoples (including their revolutions) was judged by its correspondence with the American Way. The weaker the correlation, the greater the urge to intervene to help the wayward find the proper path to freedom and prosperity. Second, the faith in America's uniqueness coupled with the failure of others to copy the perfect revolution generated a deep sense of being *alone*. Americans considered themselves perpetually beleaguered, an attitude that led on to the conviction that military security was initially to be found in controlling the entire continent—and ultimately prompted them to deny *any* distinction between domestic and foreign policy.

Here again we can learn from Weinberg, an extremely subtle historian who offers sophisticated examples of how psychology can inform our understanding of what happened in the past and of who we are in the present. He suggests, for example, that the failure to conquer Canada during the Revolutionary War transformed acquisitiveness (or greed) into a trauma of insecurity. An irrational concern for "security for the future." He then ties that to the conviction of beginning the world over again: "a feeling of preordained right to ideal security." And so, "subordinating to their own right to security another people's right to liberty and equality, Americans apparently considered that no natural right of another was inalienable upon occasion—that on which it conflicted with the always inalienable rights of Americans themselves."

But even Franklin, that sly imperialist, had the sense to set limits. "To desire the Enemies whole country," he warned in 1760, "upon no other Principle but that otherwise you cannot secure your own, is turning the Idea of mere Defence into the most dangerous of all Principles. It is leaving no medium between Safety and Conquest."

But Americans increasingly defined safety in terms of conquest—or at any rate domination.

CHAPTER FOUR

The Imperial Logic:
Land, Trade, Philosophy, and War

If we remain one people, under an efficient government, the period is not far off when . . . we may choose peace or war, as our interest, guided by justice shall counsel.

GEORGE WASHINGTON, Farewell Address, 1796

The day is within my time . . . when we may say by what laws other nations shall treat us upon the sea. And we shall say it.

THOMAS JEFFERSON, 1801

I am persuaded no constitution was ever before as well calculated as ours for extensive empire and self-government.

THOMAS JEFFERSON, 1809

A war will give us commerce and character.

HENRY CLAY, 1811

[Our system] will fit a larger empire than ever yet existed, and I have long believed that such an empire will rise in America, and give quiet to the world.

MATTHEW LYON, of Vermont and Kentucky, 1816

FOCUS your mind on three phrases: "choose peace or war, as our interest, guided by justice shall counsel"; "when we may say. . . . And we shall say it"; and "give quiet to the world." One removes war from the realm of self-defense, and the other two bespeak an assumption of omnipotence. Washington was being prudent, but he was not being anti-imperial. And, as with Washington, so with Madison. Their contemporaries read them right. After the acquisition of Louisiana and the Floridas, the opening of a window on the Pacific coast, and the revelation of the Holy Truth known as the Monroe Doctrine, John Quincy Adams indulged himself in a rare bit of understatement. Referring explicitly to Washington's observations, he offered this comment in 1826: "must we not say that the period he predicted as then not far off has arrived."*

Adams was a politician, to be sure, but he was also, in his *Diary* and *Memoirs*, a contemporary historian. Three generations later, a historian hungry for presidential power made

---

* Chapters Four through Seven are followed by an Appendix recounting the interventions of Americans overseas or beyond their borders in the North American continent.

the same point. Thomas Woodrow Wilson commented that Washington "would seem to have meant . . . 'I want you to discipline yourselves and . . . be good boys until you . . . are big enough to stand the competition . . . until you are big enough to go abroad in the world.' "

But Adams, unlike Wilson, ultimately said no to empire as a way of life. And even Jefferson recognized that there was a choice. Here we have to go back to John Taylor of Caroline County. For, whatever his imperial actions (and there were many), Jefferson was forever haunted by Taylor's critique of empire. It is easy, and in truth proper, finally to discount Jefferson's second thoughts simply because he always over-rode them and acted to sustain the imperial way of life.

But it is nevertheless important to realize that some of the masters of the empire had doubts about that *Weltanschauung*. It is not only, not even primarily, to document the existence over the years of a counter tradition. After all, the unequivocal anti-imperialists have generally been highly articulate. If rhetoric were votes, they would have won more than once. The vital point is to reveal the power of imperial logic. Or, to put it another way, which most of the anti-imperialists seldom did, what does one substitute for empire?

Jefferson and John Quincy Adams looked that question square in the eye. For the moment let us concentrate on Jefferson. One is tempted to cite him as proof of the arch-conservative argument about the dangers of a liberal education. He read so widely and thoughtfully beyond the literature of his "job" that he regularly explored strikingly different ideas. He had the courage, for example, to push his proposition about the relationship between the small freeholder and liberty to its logical conclusion: if the wide diffusion of property is the key to freedom and representative government, then should we not simply and directly redistribute property every generation?

Madison, with whom he explored the proposition, quietly

ignored such heresy, and nobody offered it as an amendment to the Constitution. That would, after all, jimmy the cornerstone of empire as a way of life. Not only did it say that enough was enough, it looked to the creation of a community to take care of those who pass their surplus property on to others in the name of community.

It is not surprising that Jefferson failed to elicit any serious support for that approach, but it is a mistake to discount it as an aberration. He also wrote another friend expressing his respect for and interest in the Chinese policy of self-containment. Perhaps Jefferson was familiar, through the tales of Marco Polo, with the story of Admiral Cheng-Hô. That remarkable leader organized and led more than five expeditions that went west to Africa, each flotilla with ships of upwards of 450 feet, and carrying some 37,000 people, decades before the Portuguese inched their way eastward around the Cape of Good Hope. The Chinese came, observed, considered the options, and then burned and otherwise destroyed their potentially imperial fleets.

In any event, Jefferson knew enough to cite the Chinese as an example of a non-imperial way of life. In a similar way, he wrestled with the issues of how to deal with the First Americans and with slavery. It is easy—for that matter, even correct—to say that Jefferson (and others) backed off from all those confrontations. But it is at least possible that the most important issues lie elsewhere.

The first involves the extreme difficulty, even in the abstract, of devising and creating an alternative to empire as a way of life. For once people begin to acquire and enjoy and take for granted and waste surplus resources and space as a routine part of their lives, and to view them as a sign of God's favor, then it requires a genius to make a career—let alone create a culture—on the basis of agreeing upon limits. Especially when several continents lie largely naked off your shores.

But, even so, it just might be done if your countrymen did not consider themselves unique, if they were not well along to paranoid conceptions of security, and if they did not believe empire was the key to freedom and self-realization. Or if, despite all that, there was in your way of life a strong commitment to community—to an acceptance of limits upon the individual in the name of the common welfare. But in a capitalist marketplace society, the ideas and ideals of community and the common welfare pose fundamental challenges to the principles of private property. Hence community can only be realized through empire that provides a surplus of property.

II

And so it is neither surprising nor damning that Jefferson turned away from redistributing property and the example of the Chinese in favor of the politics of empire. Land was crucial, but so were markets for the surpluses produced on the land. Hence, even as he moved in 1802–03 to acquire the Louisiana Territory (for commerce as well as virgin soil), he used the navy to subdue the Barbary pirates to ensure American trade in the Middle East. That campaign did not produce a major war; but it did give the Marines one phrase in the first line of their marching (and drinking) song—"From the Halls of Montezuma to the shores of Tripoli"—which perfectly symbolized the combination of wars for land and trade.

It is extremely difficult, probably impossible, to say when Jefferson abandoned his exploration of alternatives and committed himself to acquiring the entire North American continent. He was considering such plans as early as 1783, a bit later talking about an "empire for liberty" that included Canada, the Floridas, Cuba, and at least part of Mexico, and very quickly had his mind on dominating trade with Hawaii and China. And he did take Louisiana, did emphasize the importance of "the most direct and practicable communications across the continent for the purposes of commerce," and did make it clear that the citizens of Louisiana would be ruled by Washington. Those long-established people, he judged, were "as yet incapable of self-government as children."

The historian, at least this historian, is never absolutely sure about his evaluation of the evidence. We must do our best, and speak our mind. Even so, one must always wonder, as with the poets, "what if." I have just argued, for example, that Jefferson's exploration of alternatives to empire as a way of life was doomed to failure. Yet a significant minority of Americans opposed the acquisition of Louisiana, and others who approved the imperial purchase nevertheless criticized the government's arbitrary imposition of its centralized authority. There was a momentary revival of the debate over Madison's theory of imperial republicanism. In a typical exchange, Timothy Pickering of Massachusetts argued forcefully that such expansion would lead to strife, disintegration, and decline. He was answered by John Breckenridge of Kentucky, who attacked that "old and hackneyed doctrine" in the name of the majority. "So far from believing in the doctrine that a Republic ought to be confined within narrow limits, I believe the contrary, that the more extensive its dominion the more safe and durable it will be."

Breckenridge not only had the votes in the Congress, but he also correctly viewed himself as the spokesman of the dominant American tradition. Poet Philip Freneau had demanded control of the Mississippi as early as 1782: describing it as that mighty imperial waterway "in comparison of whom the Nile is but a Rivulet and the Danube a mere ditch."

Perhaps the most revealing evidence of the triumph of

Madison's imperial outlook was provided by John Quincy Adams of Massachusetts. At the risk of his political career (which he valued very highly), he broke with New Englanders like Pickering to support the acquisition of Louisiana and boldly proclaimed that America was "destined by God and nature to be the most populous and most powerful people ever combined under one social compact." His labors to realize that vision of the Lord contributed a great deal to the subsequent extension of the empire, but he also sensed the dangers inherent in such expansion.

Adams and others (including some westerners) vigorously supported the charge leveled by the citizens of Louisiana that Jefferson's actions were "inconsistent with every principle of civil liberty." Jefferson ignored Adams and the other critics. Writing privately after he took office in 1801, Jefferson committed himself to Madison's theory, and then made the vow public in his second inaugural address: "the larger our association the less it will be shaken by local passions." He became ever more strident as he moved through his second term toward retirement. Consider, for example, his comments on naval matters written for private *and* public purposes. "We begin to broach the idea that we consider the whole gulph stream as of our waters. . . . This is essential for our tranquillity and commerce. . . ."

Then, as he left office, he encapsulated the paradoxical legacy of the Revolution and the Constitution. "I am persuaded," he concluded in 1809, "that no constitution was ever before as well calculated as ours for extensive empire and self-government." The difficulties of balancing those polarities without invoking the powers of injustice and war plagued all his successors. Jeffersonian Democracy, as it came to be called, was a creature of imperial expansion. He, perhaps even more than Madison, established it as a way of life, and most Americans embraced it because it gave them personal and social rewards. It also generated even larger visions. "Our strength," Jefferson promised, "will permit us to give the law of our hemisphere."

III

In truth, however, Jefferson and others had from the outset been giving the law to the hemisphere by signing and then breaking innumerable treaties and other contracts and agreements with the First Americans, and by extending slavery as an integral part of their empire. Americans barely celebrated their victory over the British before they launched another war (1784–88), to drive the natives further westward; and in the Battle of Fallen Timbers (1794) General Anthony Wayne cleared the way into northern Ohio. Then the First Americans were pushed out of southern Indiana. Next General William Henry Harrison defeated Shawnee Chief Tecumseh at the Battle of Tippecanoe on November 7, 1811, as the prelude to a more general assault in subsequent years.

Such aggressiveness did pose a problem: how to justify extending one's own sphere into the sphere of others who had been there first and used the resources to create a viable culture. Thomas Boudlin of Virginia said it all with quiet force. "I think they are a noble, gallant, injured race. I think they have suffered nothing but wrong and injury from us." Or consider the blunt appraisal of John Randolph of Virginia, a man never noted for his sympathy for people with colored skins: "It was our own thirst for territory, our own want of moderation," that was the engine of the continual violence.

The point, of course, is that individual preferences had long before become the substance of imperial politics. Successful leaders generalize such specifics into grand philosophies. The routine lust for land, markets, or security became justifications for noble rhetoric about prosperity, liberty, and security. And thereby war. Weinberg caught that early transformation of a natural right to security into "a hysterical apprehensiveness," almost "a progressive madness." So did Henry Nash Smith, when he recognized that "the early vision of an American Empire" embodied "on the one hand the notion of empire as command of the sea, and on the other hand the notion of empire as a populous future society occupying the interior of the American continent." Or, "Empire conceived as maritime dominion presupposes American expansion westward to the Pacific."

All of those elements help us understand why Madison insisted upon the confrontation with Great Britain that produced the War of 1812. A historian can begin almost anywhere and yet emerge with an inclusive sense of how the imperial *Weltanschauung* led to war. Consider only these elements:

1. the frontiersmen and speculators coveted the land owned by the First Americans, and were only too happy to fight the British forces in Canada that they believed were encouraging resistance by those inferior peoples;

2. similar groups in the South hankered after acres claimed by the First Americans in Georgia and the Floridas;

3. westerners who blamed British commercial policy for limiting—or closing—markets for their agricultural surpluses and thereby causing a depression;

4. westerners and easterners who concluded that the British policy of the impressment of American seamen threatened their access to markets *and* their independence *and* the welfare of other Americans *and* the power of America as the lighthouse of freedom; and,

5. easterners who thought that impressment was a threat to their profits and independence.

Finally, consider Jefferson's magnificent summary of all those interests and attitudes: "If the English do not give us the satisfaction we demand, we will take Canada, which wants to enter the Union; and when, together with Canada, we shall have the Floridas, we shall no longer have any difficulties with our neighbors; *and it is the only way of preventing them.*"*

There is enough pressure there for several wars. Quite enough, surely, to initiate hostilities and to insist upon prolonged combat even after Britain had officially made known its willingness to compromise on the basic issue. We can gain an insight into that seemingly irrational behavior by considering the rhetoric, policies, and behavior of Henry Clay of Kentucky.

Clay was an impressive figure who stormed onto the national scene in 1811 and, despite being given too much to whiskey, flattery, and ambition, remained a major figure until 1850. He built his career on an understanding that Kentucky was becoming the center of the first balanced and integrated regional political economy west of Philadelphia. As ever, surplus-producing agriculture was spawning commerce, manufacturing, banking, and imperial ideology. Displaying his great flair for verbalizing the relationships between such activities, Clay put it this way in advocating a tough stand against the British. "Sir, if you wish to avoid foreign collision you had better abandon the ocean; surrender all your commerce; give up all your prosperity."

Clay was not indifferent to territorial expansion, but it was John Quincy Adams, one of Clay's major rivals for national leadership, who most neatly combined both issues. "Who shall dare," cried Adams in imperial righteousness, "to set limits to the commerce and naval power of this country?" The British Orders in Council "strike at the root of our independence." In the next breath he told London to keep its hands off Florida. That was destined to become American property.

European leaders recognized the language of empire. Tsar

* Italics added.

Alexander, for the moment engaged with Napoleon, smiled and said only that "one keeps growing bit by bit in this world." Lord Castlereagh, the British Foreign Minister who was likewise preoccupied, nevertheless, made it clear that *the* empire would accept the challenge. "If we should find you hereafter pursuing a system of encroachment upon your neighbors, what we might do defensively is another consideration."

There is humor in the scene: one empire established throughout the world solemnly invoking the principle of self-defense against an upstart rival just gaining momentum. But also a sense of doom: empire as a way of life leads only to war and more war. One has the feeling that Adams sensed and remembered and pondered that truth. But for the moment he vigorously supported the No-Transfer Resolution by which the Congress on January 15, 1811, asserted America's right to control Florida and other Spanish possessions in the western hemisphere.

Those areas were formally defined as vital to the "security, tranquillity, and commerce"—elsewhere in the document called the "destiny"—of the United States. That reference to the right to "tranquillity" not only reminds one of Weinberg's emphasis on the way in which Americans were transforming the traditional conception of security, but it was to echo down the years, most notably during 1897–98 in connection with the launching of the war against Spain. Just then, however, the Congress contented itself with alerting the world that America felt free to undertake "the temporary occupation of the [Florida] territory."

In that general context, President Madison argued powerfully for war against Great Britain. "Acquiescence in the practice and pretensions of the British Govt. is forbidden by every view that can be taken of the subject. . . . It would recolonize our commerce by subjecting it to a foreign authority. . . . Drain from us the precious metals, endanger our monied Institutions; arrest our internal improvements, and would strangle in the cradle, the manufactures which promise so vigorous a growth. Nor would the evil be confined to our commerce, our agriculture, or our manufacturers. The Ship owners & Shipbuilders and mariners must be equally sufferers."

That reference to maritime interests involved more than just an effort to engage those New Englanders who were inclined to doubt either the necessity or the wisdom of a war. America was well along in developing a global maritime outreach, and the war accelerated the creation of a navy appropriate to such commercial expansion. Domestic exports in 1811 were $45,294,000; merchant princes like Stephan Girard were accumulating vast fortunes, and 371 ocean vessels were built in that single year.

A New Englander who moved west combined those maritime and territorial aspects of empire in his evaluation of America's prospects at the end of the conflict. After fighting in the Revolution and serving as a congressman from Vermont, Matthew Lyon repeated his political success in Kentucky and then built gunboats for the war effort. The American system, he prophesied in 1816, "will fit a larger empire than ever yet existed, and I have long believed that such an empire will arise in America, and give quiet to the world."

Beyond the imperial élan of his remark, Lyon offers three other insights into the development of the expansionist way of life. He was obviously and casually assuming, *now as an internalized article of faith*, the validity of Madison's thesis of imperial republicanism. And his striking phrase, "and give quiet to the world," was a grand secular echo of the religious zeal of John Winthrop that serves also to remind us of the imperial side of the evangelical revivalism that swept like a line squall through the West prior to the War of 1812. The New England missionaries, merchants, and whalers who were already transforming Hawaii into an American outpost on the way to Asia were increasingly supported by western comrades who were preparing the ideological and material logistic support across the continent to the harbors of the Pacific Northwest.

In the broadest sense, Lyon also understood that the British victories during the war (they burned the White House, for example) meant little in the scales of empire. And, indeed, the British knew that they could not *defeat* the United States unless they remustered their veterans of the terrible battles against Napoleon for yet another major war, a prospect which interested them not at all when they evaluated the practical difficulties and the psychological and practical risks. Lyon recognized, that is, that America won the war in the fundamental strategic accounting: however grudgingly, Great Britain accepted the United States as an equal.

John Quincy Adams, who became secretary of state under James Monroe of Virginia, quickly got it all down on paper. First in a commercial treaty in 1815, then in an agreement in 1817 to equalize (and not escalate) armaments on the Great Lakes; and in 1818 a gentleman's memorandum about fishing off Newfoundland and leaving the Pacific Northwest open to the superior fecundity of Americans. Adams was a remarkably shrewd and tough negotiator, but it is wise to remember that he could play a bold hand because he held powerful cards.

And he enjoyed it all, sure in his mind that he was doing God's Will (and hoping that it would make him the next President). He admitted in 1817 that Americans were generally viewed as "a grasping and ambitious people." Two years later, in the course of pushing the Spanish into the corner of surrender over Florida and the West, he accepted the onus of empire. "Any effort on our part to reason the world out of a belief that we are ambitious will have no other effect than we add to our ambition hypocrisy." So onward to another victory. Knowing that they were unable to do so, he told the

Spanish to establish imperial power in Florida and other provinces or give them over to America. Half-way measures would serve "no other earthly purpose than as a point of annoyance." And so in the Transcontinental Treaty of 1819 the austere gentleman from Massachusetts realized Jefferson's vision by consolidating the American presence around the northern Caribbean and on to the Pacific.

IV

And then almost everyone looked south. Some did so as a way of coping with the postwar depression (1819–21); and, led by Moses and Stephen Austin, began to move into the Mexican province of Texas. A much larger number, personified and led by Clay, viewed the revolutions in Latin America—which had been triggered by the Napoleonic wars—as a golden opportunity to build an American System that would define and control the Future in the image of the American Present. His pro-revolutionary rhetoric was eminently practical: not only did he speak candidly about "our politics, our commerce, our navigation," but he was also always careful to reserve Cuba for American control.

That was the key to his outlook. Clay viewed the revolutions within a framework defined in Washington. The newly independent countries, "*whatever may be the form of the governments established.* . . . Will obey the laws of the system of the New World. . . . It is in our power to create a system of which we shall be the center and in which all South America will act with us."

Clay was the leading western spokesman of the sophisticated mercantilism espoused by those like Washington, Madison, Adams, and Albert Gallatin of Pennsylvania. Clay agreed that America as an empire required a coordinated government program to integrate finance, agriculture, manufacturing, and commerce through a continental transportation system and a systematic effort to acquire land and markets. It was essential to bind the city and the country together in one metropolis that would then function as the center of a hemispheric—even global—empire for freedom and prosperity.

Adams, who had long favored such an approach, feared that Clay's imperial enthusiasms about Latin America would upset the delicate balance between expansion and restraint that was vital to such a project—as well as to the integrity of the empire. Adams gave over to no man in his desire and determination to control North America, even to extend the influence of the United States throughout the world. But he was slowly coming to understand that the dynamics of empire led onward to oligarchy and war. He had revealed those perceptions in his fight against Jefferson's ruthless imposition of imperial control over Louisiana, and he next set himself against Clay's interventionist proposals. "We have ardent spirits for rushing into conflict," he warned, "without looking to the consequences." In a related speech, he vigorously opposed colonialism: colonies were "engines of wrong" which undercut the morality of the empire for freedom.

And so the dilemma: to expand to the optimum imperial limit without going on into the heart of darkness. Adams confronted that issue in a memorable oration on the Fourth of July in 1821; a formal speech designed to answer Clay and to clarify the consequences of endless expansion in the name of liberty. He began with an impassioned and exaggerated defense of America's uniqueness disguised as an assault on the pretensions of the British Empire, but then confronted Clay on the way to coming to terms with himself. "America goes not abroad in search of monsters to destroy. . . . She might become the dictatress of the world; she would no longer be the ruler of her own spirit."

It was a thoughtful, powerful, and essentially subversive speech. Many people who took for granted the assumptions of empire as a way of life, including later leaders like William Henry Seward and Abraham Lincoln, as well as Henry Clay, were at some date forced to come to terms with its logic. Even Adams himself. But for the time Adams remained enfolded in the spirit of empire and was unable to control the urge to extend America's power and influence. As a result, he supported President Monroe's effort to resolve the dilemma of integrating and controlling the empire, and simultaneously agitated for a bold assertion of American predominance throughout the western hemisphere.

The President's special message to the Congress of May 4, 1822, provided a definitive analysis of the issues posed by empire as a way of life, and made an urgent plea to face them squarely—"it is of the highest importance that this question be settled." In the course of that candid presentation, Monroe offered a bold restatement of Madison's theory of imperial republicanism.

"The extension of our Union over a vast territory cannot operate unfavorably to the States individually. On the contrary, it is believed that the greater the expansion, within practical limits, and it is not easy to say what are not so, the greater the advantage which the States individually will derive from it. . . . It must be obvious to all, that the further the expansion is carried, provided it be not beyond the just limit, the greater will be the freedom of action to both Governments, and the more perfect their security; and, in all other respects, the better the effect will be to the whole American people. Extent of territory, whether it be great or small, gives to a nation many of its characteristics. It marks the extent of its resources, of its population, of its physical force. It marks, in short, the difference between a great and a small power."

Setting aside the question of how much further expansion was necessary—"it does not press for a decision at this time"—Monroe then explicitly defined the "vital importance" of internal improvements. "It is only when the expansion shall be carried beyond the faculties of the General Government, so as to enfeeble its operation, to the injury of the whole, that any of the parts can be injured. The tendency, in that stage, will be to dismemberment, and not to consolidation. This danger should, therefore, be looked at with profound attention, as one of a very serious character."

The President next offered a glowing outline of the "very important" advantages to be gained from a national program to integrate the existing empire into a coherent system. It "will facilitate the operations of war . . . promote the purposes of commerce and political intelligence among the people . . . enhance the value of our vacant lands . . . the transportation of the whole of the rich productions of our country to market, would alone more than amply compensate for all the labor and expence. . . . Every power of the General Government and of the State Governments, connected with the strength and resources of the country, would be made more efficient. . . ." All in all, the benefits are "almost incalculable."

Then came the problems: the threat to property rights in such a centrally controlled program, and the consequences of stretching the powers inherent in the Constitution beyond even their most generously interpreted boundaries. Here Monroe spoke as a southerner concerned about slavery and influenced by Taylor's deep fears about losing liberty in the name of an empire for freedom. It came down to the question of whether or not the Constitution authorized the condemnation of property for public purposes. Can the Congress, asked Monroe, "summon a jury of upright and discreet men to condemn the land, value it, and compel the owner to receive the amount, and deliver it up to them? I believe that very few would concur in the opinion that such a power exists. . . . I think that it may fairly be concluded that such a right has not been granted." Hence the need for a Constitutional amendment to grant such powers to the Congress.

One can only salute Monroe (along with Adams and others) for confronting a major contradiction in empire as a way of life in a capitalist political economy. The imperatives of empire demanded the consolidation of the metropolis if it was to function as the center of empire, yet such centralization threatened the freedom promised by the empire. And if such control was not defined and exercised through public and republican processes, then it would ultimately evolve through the growth of ever greater private and bureaucratic power. Instead of private property being subjected to community purposes and controls, some private property would extend its control and purposes over most private property with the assistance of the ostensibly republican and responsible government.

Taylor had long years before warned of the *"iron government"* inherent in the Constitution, but Monroe's message of May 4, 1822, defined a moment of truth for America's imperial *Weltanschauung*. It confronted the leaders as well as the led with the opportunity to say that enough is enough, and to revise their belief that open-ended empire was the best of all possible worlds. It was, indeed, a turning point at which no one turned.

Adams had sensed that truth as he prepared his Fourth of July oration in 1821, and he later confronted the issue even more directly during the 1830s and 1840s, but in 1822–23 he sought to have it both ways. He fought for a system of national internal improvements while simultaneously asserting America's imperial authority in the western hemisphere and its right to penetrate all markets around the world.

The unilateral announcement of American predominance throughout the western hemisphere was made by the President in the course of his December 1823 annual message to the Congress and the country, and it came to be known as the Monroe Doctrine. He bluntly told all European powers that they would not be allowed to reconquer former colonies, transfer them to stronger allies, or establish new outposts of empire. Few contemporaries missed the implication: Hands Off for Europe meant Hands On for the United States. Even Adams and Clay could compromise their temperamental and pragmatic differences on the basis of that proposition.

Particularly as Monroe concurrently revealed the American inability to stay at home and cultivate its own garden. Having told Europeans to surrender the western hemisphere with dignity and grace, he then asserted the right of the United States to support Greek revolutionaries. It was not so much confusing as it was indicative of the logic of empire as a way of life: our revolution was the perfect revolution, and hence we support your effort to emulate us, and your success will extend our benevolent empire for freedom.

APPENDIX
American Interventionist Activity
(excluding declared wars) from 1787 to 1829.

1798–1800   Undeclared naval war with France. This contest included land actions, such as that in Dominican Republic, city of Puerto Plata, where marines captured a French privateer under the guns of the forts.

1801–05   Tripoli. The first Barbary war, including the *George Washington* and *Philadelphia* affairs and the Eaton expedition, during which a few marines landed with United States Agent William Eaton to raise a force against Tripoli in an effort to free the crew of the *Philadelphia*.

1806   Mexico (Spanish territory). Capt. Z. M. Pike, with a platoon of troops, invaded Spanish territory at the headwaters of the Rio Grande deliberately and on orders from Gen. James Wilkinson.

1806–10   Gulf of Mexico. American gunboats operated from New Orleans against Spanish and French privateers, such as LaFitte, off the Mississippi delta, chiefly under Capt. John Shaw and Master Commandant David Porter.

1810   West Florida (Spanish territory). Governor Claiborne of Louisiana, on orders of the President, occupied with troops, territory in dispute east of Mississippi as far as the Pearl River, later the eastern boundary of Louisiana. He was authorized to seize as far east as the Perdido River. No armed clash.

1812   Amelia Island and other parts of East Florida, then under Spain. Temporary possession was authorized by President Madison and by Congress, to prevent occupation by any other power; but possession was obtained by Gen. George Matthews in so irregular a manner that his measures were disavowed by the President.

1813   West Florida (Spanish territory). On authority given by Congress, General Wilkinson seized Mobile Bay in April with 600 soldiers. A small Spanish garrison gave way. Thus we advanced into disputed territory to the Perdido River, as projected in 1810. No fighting.

1813–14   Marquesas Islands. Built a fort on island of Nukahiva to protect three prize ships which had been captured from the British.

1814   Spanish Florida. Gen. Andrew Jackson took Pensacola and drove out the British with whom the United States was at war.

1814–25 Caribbean. Engagements between pirates and American ships or squadrons took place repeatedly especially ashore and offshore about Cuba, Puerto Rico, Santo Domingo, and Yucatan. In 1822 Commodore James Biddle employed a squadron of two frigates, four sloops of war, two brigs, four schooners, and two gunboats in the West Indies.

1815 Algiers. The second Barbary war, declared by our enemies but not by the United States. Congress authorized an expedition. A large fleet under Decatur attacked Algiers and obtained indemnities.

1815 Tripoli. After securing an agreement from Algiers, Decatur demonstrated with his squadron at Tunis and Tripoli, where he secured indemnities for offenses against us during the War of 1812.

1816 Spanish Florida. United States forces destroyed Nicholls Fort, called also Negro Fort, because it harbored raiders into United States territory.

1816–18 Spanish Florida. First Seminole war. The Seminole Indians, whose area was a resort for escaped slaves and border ruffians, were attacked by troops under Generals Jackson and Gaines and pursued into northern Florida. Spanish posts were attacked and occupied. British citizens executed.

1817 Amelia Island (Spanish territory off Florida). Under orders of President Monroe, United States forces landed and expelled a group of smugglers, adventurers, and freebooters.

1818 Oregon. The U.S.S. *Ontario*, dispatched from Washington, landed at the Columbia River and in August took possession.

1820–26 Africa. Naval units raided the slave trade pursuant to the 1819 act of Congress.

1822　Cuba. United States naval forces suppressing piracy landed on the northwest coast of Cuba and burned a pirate station.

1823　Cuba. Brief landings in pursuit of pirates occurred April 8 near Escondido; April 16 near Cayo Blanco; July 11 at Siquapa Bay; July 21 at Cape Cruz; and October 23 at Camrioca.

1823　Cuba. In October the U.S.S. *Porpoise* landed bluejackets near Matanzas in pursuit of pirates. This was during the cruise authorized in 1822.

1824　Puerto Rico (Spanish territory). Commodore David Porter with a landing party attacked the town of Pajardo which had sheltered pirates and insulted American naval officers. He landed with 200 men in November and forced an apology.

1825　Cuba. In March cooperating American and British forces landed at Sagua La Grande to capture pirates.

1827　Greece. In October and November landing parties hunted pirates on the islands of Argenteire, Miconi, and Androsa.

CHAPTER FIVE
More Freedom and More Empire

The prosperity . . . The splendour, and . . . the duration of the Empire.

ADAM SMITH, 1754

There has never been a constitution or government, which admitted such an indefinite and unlimited extension of territory or population as our own—nay, more, which so required extension for success.

WILLIAM W. GREENOUGH,
Boston merchant, 1849

We Americans are the peculiar, chosen people—the Israel of our time.

HERMAN MELVILLE, 1850

I chant the new empire.

WALT WHITMAN, 1860

But I reckon I got to light out for the territory ahead of the rest, because Aunt Sally she's going to adopt me and civilize me, and I can't stand that.

HUCKLEBERRY FINN, 1884

Not the Constitution, but free land and an abundance of natural resources open to a fit people, made the democratic type of society in America for three centuries.

FREDERICK JACKSON TURNER, 1920

HISTORIANS of every persuasion agree that the election of Andrew Jackson in 1828 symbolized and accelerated a shift in American culture. Surely they are correct about the *perception* of reality among the people of that era: even Jackson's critics felt themselves to be experiencing a sea change, and most people were certain that they were freer. And many white Americans did move hither and yon, geographically and socially, with a flair approaching abandon.

But then the issues become less clear. Far from improving, the lives of blacks and First Americans became increasingly difficult and painful. In the broader sense, moreover, force or the threat of force became routinely deployed in *domestic* affairs as well as in foreign policy. As for the *Weltanschauung*, the evidence is unequivocal: empire remained the American Way of Life.

The major historical idiom for discussing and evaluating these matters centers on the change from mercantilism to laissez-faire. The American version and practice of that shift in outlook is different from the one in Europe, but the fundamental proposition is sound. We are dealing with the transition from a state-building—hence more centralized, organized, controlled, even partially planned—kind of capitalism to a far more individualistic, random, free-marketplace capitalism. That perspective is informative as long as we do not forget that in the game of cultural change the winners usually discount or deny the wisdom they have stolen from the losers.

Free-enterprise capitalism did *not* abjure—let alone abandon—The State. It merely used it in different ways. The vaunted individual entrepreneur continued to rely upon funds supplied by his fellow taxpayers. We do not need, at least not here, to dwell upon all the direct and indirect public subsidies that have funded the toll ways, the canals, the railroads, the automobile industry, the airlines, and other business ventures. Let us instead go back to the patron saint of laissez-faire, free-enterprise capitalism. His name was Adam Smith, and he was far more candid than most of his followers. Indeed, he was a Scot who was refreshingly outspoken about three crucial matters.

First, Smith acknowledged (in his masterpiece *The Wealth of Nations*) the achievement, even the necessity, of the organized kind of capitalism known as mercantilism. He admitted that the Anglo-Saxon-Americans could not have wriggled upward from the muck of backwardness and underdevelopment without such a common effort coordinated and directed by a strong central government. He next emphasized that an active State was essential to ensure the domestic success of laissez-faire capitalism: to underwrite education, to ensure law and order, and to control the giants that would inevitably arise under the conditions of free competition.

Third, Smith repeatedly underscored the vital importance of The State in expanding the marketplace. His entire system was predicated upon unending growth—upon empire. *Smith's argument with the mercantilists was about means—not ends*. He wholly agreed with the mercantilists about the necessity of expansion. His objective was the same, and he described it with great verve: "the prosperity . . . the splendour, and . . . the duration of the Empire."

Marx took Smith very seriously, and in this instance characterized the dynamics of laissez-faire capitalism with great dramatic flair. "The need for a constantly expanding market for its products chases the bourgeoisie over the whole surface of the globe. It must nestle everywhere, settle everywhere, establish connections everywhere. . . . Have intercourse in every direction, universal inter-dependence of nations . . . . [Capitalism] compels all nations, on pain of extinction, to adopt the bourgeois mode of production; it compels them to introduce what it calls civilization into their midst . . . . In one word, it creates a world after its own image." Magnificent; but, even so, let us remember the words Smith used to define the purpose of laissez-faire: "the prosperity . . . the splendour, and . . . the duration of the Empire."

I

Andrew Jackson was an orphan who became a lawyer who became a land speculator who became a charismatic killer of First American Braves and British Regulars who became President. Jackson shared Smith's objectives—and in his own way honored Smith's means. He approved of The State helping small as well as upwardly mobile capitalists; and hence opposed a national, centrally directed program for internal improvements in favor of local, almost casual contracts for roads and canals. And he destroyed the existing national monetary system to open the arena to local banks—whatever their weaknesses and irresponsibilities. It was a rough-and-ready kind of laissez-faire that released enormous energy and generated great enthusiasm even as it produced serious economic and social problems.

As with Smith, Jackson accepted empire as a way of life. And there is no denying, at least in some respects, that such expansion is democratic. The combination of surplus resources plus surplus space plus a lack of central control does give many people a greater opportunity to vote their cussedness, claim more land, and move on after a failure to try again and again. The majority of whites naturally concluded that there was no better definition of freedom, liberty, and The Truth.

But the system has certain structural weaknesses, such as an inherent cycle of boom and bust, and an internal logic that works to concentrate even more power in ever fewer hands. It also faces the fundamental dilemma of empire: a moment of truth that arrives when people who accept the principles of the system threaten its further expansion. Jackson confronted two such crises: with the First Americans who reluctantly but honestly embraced the European definition of civilization; and with his compatriots in South Carolina who acted on the axiom of pursuing their own interests. And then came another crunch; the challenge of how to expand the empire, increasingly considered sacred as well as necessary, without subverting the ideals of liberty, freedom, and perpetual opportunity.

The action of South Carolina to nullify the high tariff legislation of 1828 and 1832, undertaken in the economic and political interests of its agricultural system, was formally a domestic issue. And Jackson's moves to assert national power could be—and were—defended within the principles of Smithian laissez-faire. Even so, the confrontation provides two insights into the evolving psychology of empire as a way of life.

One concerns the speed and militance of Jackson's response. Granted the President's hypersensitive ego and his propensity to violence, his actions revealed a great fear about the stability of the system which was clearly tied to the conviction that empire was necessary to the American way of life. And that, in turn, was intimately related to what Weinberg has described as the early and steady movement "toward a hysterical apprehensiveness" about security.

For, even as bargaining maneuvers, Jackson's rhetoric about South Carolina leaving the Union as incipient treason, and his military preparations, revealed a fundamental tendency to overreact and to engage in the kind of gross distortion and exaggeration that easily becomes a self-fulfilling prophecy. As in many subsequent confrontations involving the United States, the conflict could have been resolved in a far more relaxed manner.

The First Americans had earlier discovered, however, that in matters pertaining to empire the European invaders were not at all relaxed. By the time Jackson was elected, most of the natives in the Northeast and Great Lakes region had either been destroyed, pushed out of their homelands, or reduced to a desperately weakened condition. Jackson promptly provided help to finish them off in the southeastern part of the country.

There are two particularly important aspects of this imperial episode. First, it is a mistake to personalize it around the President. He was important, but not crucial: the highly acclaimed symbol of a widespread antagonism toward the First Americans and a visceral determination to acquire their land, other resources, and space. Secondly, and unlike the confrontation with South Carolina, the government's action involved a clear violation of its avowed commitment to the principles of a laissez-faire political economy.

To begin with, the Cherokees, Creeks, Choctaws, and Chickasaws held title to their land through treaties with the government. The Cherokees, furthermore, had accepted a fundamentally paternalistic compromise devised by Madison and other predecessors of Jackson. In return for reorganizing their political economy on European principles—based on non-nomadic agriculture—the Cherokees would be left alone to honor their own way of life. Though certainly not perfectly equitable, and infused with considerable secular and religious fervor to civilize the Cherokees, it was a workable arrangement within the philosophy of allowing and encouraging people to pursue their self-interest.

The Cherokees displayed an impressive ability to adapt to those conditions, and a flair for economic and political innovation that produced a functioning culture within their allotted acres. Increasing numbers of Georgians, and other white southerners, became ever more envious of, and upset by, that success. Not only did it deny them an excuse to take the land because it was not being used in the proper manner, but it struck at the cornerstone of their myth about the inherent and permanent inferiority of people with colored skin. (They were also disturbed to discover that some Cherokees were blue-eyed blonds.) Simply put, the Cherokees proved effective farmers who governed themselves in a representative and peaceful manner.

A few southerners, and some northerners, recognized that achievement and resisted the pressure to remove the Cherokees across the Mississippi. John Quincy Adams, for example, felt that, while they were surely doomed, they must not be displaced without their consent. He enforced that view while he was President (1825–29), but in 1830 Jackson and others approved legislation that authorized the removal of the Cherokees with or without their agreement.

Those brave people put their trust in the courts, and in 1831 Chief Justice John Marshall ruled in their favor. But Jackson imperially refused to honor or enforce the decision, and by 1838 the Cherokees had been driven westward across the Mississippi in a cruel winter march that killed men, women, and children without prejudice. Alabama and Mississippi followed Georgia's lead, as did the northerners who defeated the Sauk and Fox Nations, and by the 1850s the

First Americans had been removed from the eastern half of the continent.

II

By the time the Cherokees (and others) had begun to reestablish themselves in the West they were outflanked to the south, increasingly threatened to the north, and about to be closeted to the west. They would survive another sixty years, but largely because the white Americans were temporarily distracted by other imperial enterprises. The first of those involved simultaneously wrapping-up the last benefit of the War of 1812 and acquiring by conquest the northern half of Mexico. That triumphant extension of the empire cannot be understood, however, simply in terms of the pressures to add the Oregon Territory and Texas as part of the process of what Jackson liked to call "extending the area of freedom."

The imperial way of life, as should now be apparent, involved many kinds of economic factors as well as politics, ideas, and psychology. But no historian has yet dramatized the story of how Americans began, even before they acquired Louisiana, to view the ocean as their next frontier. Despite the insights of such perceptive scholars as Henry Nash Smith, Richard W. Van Alstyne, and Norman Graebner, we have little more than bits and pieces as yet not integrated into a comprehensive account. Jefferson's concern to control the Pacific Northwest was not even the beginning of the story.

By the end of the Revolution, American merchants and traders were sending their ships on far voyages into the Pacific, as well as to Europe and Latin America. While some New Englanders concentrated on fishing off the northeastern shores, others stalked seals and whales in the South Atlantic, the Antarctic, and the Pacific. And by the 1820s others were shipping cowhides from Spanish California to be made into shoes for the descendants of the Puritans. Those ships also carried missionaries who discovered that the Lord's will (and their welfare) could be furthered by marrying heathen females who were in line to inherit large tracts of real estate in Hawaii. Those theological pioneers—we shall be as a city upon a volcano—were energetic, happy, and successful in the fields of the Lord; and by the late 1830s had established themselves as the effective power in the Hawaiian islands.

As Boston merchant William Sturgis admitted, the men of maritime affairs were no less "covetous and ambitious" than the entrepreneurs on land. The pursuit of self-interest was amphibian. The navy, for example, asserted in 1829 that all west coast harbors belonged to the United States. Captain David Porter returned from the first official foray into the Pacific (1812–13) to lobby for more support, and he and his commercial allies were effective. The government established a South American Squadron in 1821, and by 1835 had ships on station in the Far East.

The size and cannon power of those flotillas is far less important than the imperial energy and commitment they symbolized. Three years later, strongly encouraged by Representative John N. Reynolds of New York and other maritime spokesmen, the navy was authorized in the person of Charles Wilkes to explore the frontier of the sea, including the possibility that one could sail inside the earth after finding ports of entry at either pole. Whatever its difficulties, even absurdities, the venture produced charts used by the navy as late as the 1940s war against Japan.

That kind of holes-in-the-poles romantic nonsense was not limited to naval officers. Novelist James Fenimore Cooper, an ardent supporter of President Jackson, wrote marvelously imperial sea stories in which every ship was sleek and every sailor was handsome. Even Herman Melville had trouble deciding whether he was for or against empire. He could attack the "lack of historical sense" of his fellow citizens (as in

Mardi), and then proclaim America as a "political Messiah" (as in *White Jacket*). Reading all that literature, one has the feeling that the sea was the only phenomenon that empire as a way of life could not quite encompass.

But most Americans, leaders as well as led, seem to have agreed with George Bancroft, the Jacksonian enthusiast who became the first secretary of the navy and the founding spirit of the Naval Academy at Annapolis. The sea, cried Bancroft, was another frontier whereupon America would extend "the glad tidings of the Gospel . . . [and] the American Revolution," and open "a new and more glorious ear" for humankind. Bancroft was a romantic, to be sure, but he did not create the Naval Academy simply—or even primarily —to train seaborne secular evangelists. He and countless others were after the resources, the commerce, and the markets.

The merchants were reaping huge profits from Baltimore clippers and their tall-masted offspring. Those magnificent ships, visually glamorous but harsh seafaring, generated as much money as horsepower. They were the means to fortunes in the trade around South America and on westward to Asia, and created the presence that led on to influence in China, and ultimately prompted Commodore Matthew C. Perry's imperial show of force at Yedo Bay and Yokohama, Japan. Even the statistics are impressive: American exports jumped from $52.6 million in 1815 to more than $400 million in 1860.

Asa Whitney of New York was another statistic. He was a wealthy man who went bankrupt in the Panic of 1837 (and the ensuing depression), then sailed off to Asia and returned in 1844 with another fortune. He could also translate statistics into imperial rhetoric and policy. "Here we stand forever, we reach out one hand to all Asia, and the other to all Europe, willing for all to enjoy the great blessings we possess, . . . but all . . . tributary, and at our will subject to us." But one did not have to go to Asia to embrace trans-oceanic empire.

Consider only Thomas Hart Benton of Missouri, a dedicated Jacksonian. He always insisted, with good reason, that he became an imperialist at the knee of Thomas Jefferson. Ever westward to The Truth. "Access to Asia becomes a symbol of freedom and of national greatness." Also the trail "to the highest pinnacle of wealth and power, and with it the higher attainments of letters, arts, and sciences." (There was the rationale for many decisions made a century later.)

A nod further south, Robert J. Walker of Mississippi was a bit more prosaic. America can never realize its "great destiny" unless it commands "the market of more than thousand millions of people. . . . The markets and the commerce of the world." Lest anyone think that empire was a fantasy generated by the heat and humidity of the South, consider only Stephen A. Douglas of Illinois. His passion for a transcontinental railway was no doubt niggled by his personal investments, but he was after "the vast commerce of the Pacific Ocean." And he was aware that western farmers, like their eastern and southern counterparts, wanted another outlet for their surplus production.

But there were ideological and psychological, as well as economic, surpluses, and they also sought markets. The intellectuals were overproducing imperial ideas and rhetoric. Walt Whitman, that poet of the common man, declared that expansion generated "unparalleled human happiness and national freedom." Ralph Waldo Emerson concluded that "our whole history appears to be a last effort of Divine Providence on behalf of the human race." Along with Bancroft, such giants as William Prescott, John Lathrop Motley, and Francis Parkman glorified empire as adventure. Even as conquest.

The ultimately magic phrase, "manifest destiny," was coined by John L. O'Sullivan, editor of the *Democratic Re-*

view. In many ways, however, the materials of the mash that produced that 200-proof imperial snort are even more revealing of empire as a way of life. America, O'Sullivan explained, constitutes "the beginning of a new history . . . which separates us from the past and connects us with the future only." "Who will, what can, set limits to our onward march." Our mission is "to smite unto death the tyranny of kings, hierarchs, and oligarchs, and carry the glad tidings of peace and good will where myriads now endure an existence scarcely more enviable than the beasts of the field." America is "the Great Nation of Futurity."

It *is* bold. It is candidly, even gloriously, imperial. Let us accept that: an honest imperialist is surely preferable to an apologetic, let alone a disingenuous, imperialist. But perhaps it is too bold. It reminds one more than a bit of James Fenimore Cooper and his hero Natty Bumpo. So bold as to be straining for a legitimacy not inherent in the action. One thinks here of the comments by George Sand, and later Martin Green. Sand first whispered the truth about Natty's efforts to deal with "power acquired at the cost of suffering, murder, and fraud." Green spoke more bluntly and directly: "a moral hero who performs immoral acts, so his moral life has to be all in his speeches. . . . He has to rationalize everything he does."

III

And there was, and continues to be, much rationalization about the conquest of Mexico. Historians have also debated the issue of whether the war was primarily concerned with territorial or maritime objectives. The argument provides a good example of the fallacy of misplaced concreteness because it is not an either-or question. Texas was a territorial issue, and without Texas there would have been no war. The concern with land and other resources was clear and explicit, and the traditional idioms were repeatedly invoked in support of war. One citizen offered this paraphrase of Madison: "personal liberty is incompatible with a crowded population." Walker preferred another ancient metaphor: Texas would serve "as a safety valve" for social discontent. President James K. Polk chose to echo Monroe: "Our system may be safely extended to the utmost bounds of our territorial limits and . . . as it shall be extended the bonds of our Union, so far from being weakened, will be stronger."

As Polk's language suggests, he and others wanted more than just Texas. In particular, control of the Pacific coast from San Diego to San Francisco. But farmers as well as merchants (and other maritime interests), as well as farsighted imperial thinkers, sought to acquire those ports for "the vast commerce of the Pacific Ocean." To say nothing of the gold and agricultural properties. And some members of all those groups seemed terrified lest America might have to learn to live with an equal as a neighbor—the ever-creeping paranoia about perfect security. All those concerns were easily subsumed, and justified, à la Natty Bumpo, within the traditional mystique of mission. Walt Whitman was typically enthusiastic: "Yes, Mexico must be thoroughly chastized."

The coming of the war dramatized what John Taylor had called *"iron government."* Polk manipulated the country into violence. There was a fine irony in all of that. Taylor had centered his fears on the likes of John Adams, but it was John Quincy Adams who invoked Taylor against Polk. The President, he charged, had engaged in the "unscrupulous suppression" of information; manipulations that "prove how utterly insufficient the reservation of the power of declaring war to Congress is as a check upon the will of the President." Adams spoke for a significant minority that opposed the war, but he and his allies could not alter the imperial *Weltanschauung*.

Beyond the acquisitive and messianic forces that produced

the war, the crucial aspect of the assault on Mexico involved the further evolution of a truly imperial strategy, and the effective coordination of land and naval power to carry through the conquest. Americans had been fumbling for such an approach ever since the attack on Canada during the Revolution. Their subsequent effort to isolate and devour western Canada during the War of 1812 failed largely because they allowed their ambitions to define their plan. They moved directly on what they wanted (the West) instead of seizing what would isolate the object of their lust. Even so, they recovered from the early defeat to secure control of the Great Lakes and so won a strategic victory.

The lesson was applied in Mexico. The army, led by General Winfield Scott, and marvelously supported by the navy, bypassed the desired real estate to strike at the heart of the society. It was brilliant: threaten Mexico City in order to acquire the northern half of the country. Beyond that, it was the crucial step in developing a strategy based on confronting the enemy with a choice between annihilation or unconditional surrender. Or both.

And both defined the North's strategy against the South during the Civil War. There are many ways to analyze and explain that gory conflict, and all of them have been explored with varying degrees of sophistication and persuasiveness. My approach here is to place the war in the context of an imperial *Weltanschauung* in an era of laissez-faire capitalism. Within that framework, the campaign of conquest against Mexico led inexorably to the Civil War. For in a peaceful political and economic competition to control the new acquisition, the superior population and resources of the northern states ensured their ultimate victory. Along with a good many other leaders, southern as well as northern, Abraham Lincoln understood that truth about the dynamics of the political economy. But Lincoln publicly avowed it as his *policy*. Contain the South, prevent it from expanding, and it would wither and die. Thus southerners not illogically concluded that secession offered them the most likely chance to sustain the South *as the South*. Being expansionists, they understood the logic of empire: no growth implies death. From their point of view, the abolitionist direct assault on slavery offered dramatic proof of the accuracy of their analysis. Be destroyed slowly by Lincoln or cataclysmically by the crusaders.

One of the most fascinating aspects of the situation is that a significant number of northern anti-slavery people, typified by John Quincy Adams, also supported—even advocated—secession. Their particular arguments varied, but the substance was the same: let the South go. Or, for that matter, let the North leave first. That approach was quite in keeping with the principles of the Declaration of Independence, arguably within the logic of the Constitution, and inherent in the philosophy of laissez-faire advanced by Adam Smith.

The rigor of that position was then and later confused, and often evaded, by raising the question of slavery. Despite its long history, including the considerable achievements of societies which practiced it, slavery is evil. But that truth fails to define either the question or the answer. *For so is empire.* The irreducible issue is whether or not one uses one evil, empire, to destroy another evil, slavery.

The most sympathetic and understanding defense of Lincoln hangs on that moral and pragmatic confrontation. The imperial war for freedom. That approach allows us to set aside, without dismissing them, all the neurological, physiological, and psychological speculation about Lincoln in order to concentrate on the context in which those factors may or may not have operated. We can thus see him as a man, whatever his physical or psychic traumas, who gradually but unavoidably recognized that he had lost the bargain he had made with the Devil.

Yes, I am suggesting, in all seriousness, that Lincoln was

the first major American leader who was truly a Faustian figure. A case can be made that one or another of the Founding Fathers earned that honor. On balance, Thomas Jefferson appears to be the most promising candidate, but in reality the Sage of Monticello was too soft and too evasive. He always backed away from—or, perhaps more accurately, simply bypassed—the ultimate confrontation. Not so with Lincoln.

There is no cause to belabor the questions of Lincoln's ambition or his explicit formulation of that hunger. He wanted to surpass, transcend, the achievement of the Revolutionary and Founding Fathers. Nor need we quibble about his chosen means: to assert northern supremacy and thereby destroy the southern culture based on slavery.* His bargain with the Devil involved achieving power in the North by camouflaging, dissembling his true purposes, and then carrying through a quick victory even if the South seceded. Such a prompt, relatively bloodless triumph would give him all he sought: power, fame, and the ultimate demise of slavery. But it began to go sour almost at once. Small wonder that he became increasingly prone to dreams about his death. It was the only way out.

Lincoln's realization that the Devil called the tune, sometimes called his maturation, began when he recognized that a large number of people in the North were exceedingly reluctant to die to establish an imperial system. And that the southerners would fight very hard to sustain their independence. Thus it is particularly revealing to watch Lincoln deploy his unusual intelligence and powers of persuasion to convince northerners to leave hearth and home to embrace a

---

*I first suggested this approach to Lincoln in *America Confronts a Revolutionary World: 1776–1976* (New York: William Morrow, 1976), pp. 70–71, 89–91, and Ch. 6. The argument has recently been developed in highly formal terms by George B. Forgie, *Patricide in the House Divided: A Psychological Interpretation of Lincoln and His Age* (New York: Norton, 1979). Also see David Brion Davis, "Uncle Oedipus and Ante Bellum," *The New York Review of Books*, October 25, 1979.

bullet, stop a cannon ball, or play host to an equally deadly germ.

The President was extremely good, for example, in sermonizing about the mystique of The Union. But upon close examination (as in analyzing his annual message of December 1862), The Union materializes as blunt talk about the economic need to control the Mississippi Valley and a desperate concern for security defined as the absence of strong neighbors. Lincoln had to win quickly, and hence by that date he was talking candidly because time was running out.

For if he did not zap the Confederacy, then the Devil would call the loan and all hell would break loose. He might easily lose the election of 1864; but, even if he remained in the White House, there would be no quiet Second Revolution. The reins of empire as a way of life were slipping from his hands. The evil of empire proved a demon. And so it became a ruthless war of annihilation—which inevitably led on to a period of occupation and colonial rule.

Nobody has told that part of the story as well as Russel F. Weigley in his unnerving study *The American Way of War*. Weigley plays it low key, saying that "Lincoln acquiesced" in the consequences. But the President had no choice. He had rolled snake eyes with the Devil, and it was over. There was nothing to do but see it through. So he "matured" while Generals John Pope, Ulysses S. Grant, and William T. Sherman ravaged a people and their culture. And they established, even without the excuse of revenge for similar acts, the strategic tradition of destroying the opponent's society that caused so much trouble—and horror—in America's later wars.

IV

That approach was next used against the First Americans west of the Mississippi. The much acclaimed peaceful side of the strategy of annihilation was based on the threat of force to break the will of those people by isolating them within ever smaller, and less supportive, areas of land and resources called reservations. That was the reduction to farce of the old bargain with the Cherokees: give them a space which could not support them—and then implacably reduce the space. The violent aspect, devised and implemented by Generals Sherman, Philip H. Sheridan, and George A. Custer, called for overpowering assaults on the First Americans during the winter months when they were most vulnerable. It was brilliant imperial strategy and miserable morality.

But it was pretty much a horror sideshow. The great thrust for empire concerned going abroad for markets, resources, and various benighted peoples to enlighten and redeem. As that movement emerged and developed power, the territorial empire consolidated by the destruction of the Confederacy provided varying kinds and degrees of freedom and opportunity for the citizenry. The slaves were free, though their options were desperately circumscribed by their lack of education, capital, and mobility, and by the system of racial discrimination and intimidation that emerged after the period of northern occupation. The vast majority of ex-slaves were jammed down into the underclass of sharecropping where politics was defined by survival rather than competition for wealth and power. The idea of equal opportunity in an open marketplace was at best a grim joke in their poetry.

Many white southerners fared little better as marginal farmers or urban workers. But a large number of northerners (even among the influx of immigrants) did improve their condition—at least now and again. Back and mind-breaking labor, among women and children as well as men, enabled them to keep their land or industrial jobs. And some wriggled their way upward into the entrepreneurial middle class.

A much smaller group of whites, including some southerners, enjoyed the capital, skills, ruthlessness, and luck to move up the ladder of laissez-faire capitalism as if it were an escalator. They gained power as well as money. Understandably, they spoke often, forcefully, and even sometimes eloquently, about the reality of freedom and opportunity. And, for a time, they were confident that empire as a way of life had been vindicated. Not at all atypically, Senator James R. Doolittle of Wisconsin put it this way: the surplus of free land "will postpone for centuries, if it will not forever, all serious conflict between capital and labor."

Even today, Doolittle could make a strong argument that he had been correct. Particularly if we grant him the way in which continental empire was transformed into a global empire. For, despite all the troubles that appeared in his lifetime, and later, there has been no revolution generated by the conflict between capital and labor. Part of the explanation involves nothing more mysterious than the size and natural wealth of the continental empire, and the raw energy (and elementary necessities) of a rapidly growing population.

Treating those factors as given, and ignoring the realities of empire, the philosophers and propagandists of laissez-faire capitalism celebrate it all as proof of their revelation. It is a beguiling, touching faith, redolent with all manner of sacred texts, hierarchies, ceremonies, and rationalization, and particularly persuasive in the absence of serious history. But few leaders or members of the church take any of it seriously as a guide to action at any given moment. They do not want to be left alone to their own devices in the free marketplace. They want all the help they can get—especially from that Old Debil imperial government. Indeed, they display an impressive ability to define more freedom as more empire.

In America, moreover, that has generally held true for workers, and small and medium businesspeople, as well as for the giants. There have always been exceptions. There still are exceptions. It is furthermore conceivable that the minority will become the majority. And their history is important in its own right, as well as a source of often vibrant and powerful heresy. But the history of the United States is not the story of triumphant anti-imperial heretics. It is the account of the power of empire as a way of life, as a way of avoiding the fundamental challenge of creating a humane and equitable community or culture.

Thus the essence of American history during the generation after the Civil War concerns the way that one conception of empire was replaced by another. There are many ways to approach that process, but here I want to do it by examining two basic groups: the people who enjoyed power and influence on a routine basis, and those who were struggling to have a say in the decisions that affected everyone's life. Each group was divided within itself, and each influenced the other. Sometimes in surprising ways. Some people in both groups resisted a global re-definition of empire as a way of life, while others (in the end a majority) favored projecting the traditional concept throughout the world.

By the end of the century, a majority of both groups either favored or acquiesced in the new conception of empire. That does not mean, and I emphasize the point, that each group accepted the other's conception—or its proposed distribution of the spoils—of the new imperial *Weltanschauung*. Those matters would be vigorously debated well into the 20th century. But the majority did choose empire over any other option that was offered by anybody.

The evidence very strongly indicates that the agricultural majority of the population, largely composed of small to medium-sized dirt farmers, was the dynamic element in the shift from continental to overseas empire. However paradoxical it may appear, the essence of it is simple: the American farmer was a capitalist businessman whose welfare depended upon free access to a global marketplace, and who increasingly demanded that the government use its powers to ensure such freedom of opportunity.

A few of the people who went west did so to commune

with Nature à la Thoreau. Other small groups sought to explore the possibility of an agrarian-based communitarianism or socialism. And it can be argued that in the beginning a sizable number sought nothing more than a modestly better life as members of small local communities. But once they moved beyond the subsistence level of farming they found themselves in a highly competitive surplus-producing marketplace economy that increasingly operated as part of a world system. Of necessity if not by choice, those business families (women and children were essential to success) became ever more concerned with markets for their surplus grain, fiber, and meat, and with more land and better machines.

They were troubled by the post Civil War economic readjustment, and next hit hard by the depression that, beginning in 1873, staggered the entire economy. But then a major decline in European agriculture, caused largely by poor weather and related diseases, provided them with a vast market. It not only saved the farmers, but played a vital part in pulling the entire economy out of the depression. The psychological and political consequences were equally important: the farmers came to view themselves as *the* dynamic element in the system—no farms, no cities—and demanded recognition and active support.

That experience, and the related attitudes and beliefs, became crucial as European governments moved to protect their own farmers against the socially disruptive influx of American surpluses. The American agricultural capitalists argued that they desperately needed to maintain those outlets, even to open new ones in Latin America, Asia, and elsewhere. The equation between overseas markets and freedom had been recognized and accepted as the New Truth. The farmers launched a campaign to force Washington to protect and expand their global marketplace. Not surprisingly, they maintained that their freedom as well as their survival (as the majority of the population) depended upon such vigorous, even forceful diplomacy. They likewise attacked the Europeans and others as being autocratic—and worse—for erecting barriers against their surpluses. The old equation that defined the British, the First Americans, the Spaniards, and the Mexicans as undemocratic threats to American territorial security and welfare was thus projected onto the global scene.

There were other solutions to the problem, such as cooperatives and diversification, or even an imaginative form of socialism, and a few farmers advocated those alternatives. They gained some strength by the end of the 1880s, largely because the railroads and the bankers became so rapacious as to rival foreigners as dangers to freedom and opportunity. But the American agricultural tradition, save for a few exceptions during the early colonial years, was viscerally and fiercely capitalist: private property was the key to personal identity and freedom, and to effective, responsible government.

One leading expansionist of the Ohio River Valley caught the spirit in this remark. "Never forget that we are the only people on earth whose farmers buy the adjoining farm before they need it. We are of the blood which furnishes the world with its Daniel Boones, its Francis Drakes, its Cecil Rhodes." The freedom-loving farmers were by no means immune to the racist germ in that comment, but they were more receptive to the virus of certainty about their own virtue. They were sure that they could, given the economic and political power, save anybody anywhere. And, as children of empire, they were classically illustrative of what Wright Morris has called "the prevailing tendency of the American mind to take to the woods"—to evade any serious, ongoing confrontation with basic problems.

One of America's most insightful (though currently neglected) historians peered deeply into that paradox of

freedom-loving farmers sustaining empire as
People who open and settle the frontiers, not
Becker, "must be always transforming the wo.
ideal of it." The mind of such a people, he conti
sure of itself to be at home with ideas of uncerta
Knowing that it is right, it wishes only to go aheac. Satisfied
with certain conventional premises, it hastens on to the obvious conclusion." Becker gives us, in those few but remarkable words, the ultimate explanation of why empire as a way
of life did not end with the conquest of the continent and the
annihilation of the Confederacy.

The agricultural majority would have projected empire out
across the seven seas even if they had organized themselves
well enough to take control of the government. The most
militant leaders of those years, from Thomas E. Watson of
Georgia to Jeremiah (Sockless Jerry) Simpson of Kansas, per-
sistently expressed a fierce determination to control world
markets, and supported the campaign for a powerful navy.
"Our form of government," explained Ignatius Donnelly of
Minnesota, "is adapted to civilized man everywhere. . . .
Great as we are, we are yet in the day of small things. . . .
[Our] destiny is to grasp the commerce of all the seas and
sway the sceptre of the world." Henry Demarest Lloyd, a
vigorous activist for domestic reforms, was even blunter: "If
nobody can lick us, we need not be afraid to play the just
and generous big brother among the nations." That was the
only way, he added a bit later, "to fulfill our mission to
defend and *extend* liberty." The majority of the farmers
wanted reform at home *and* a vigorous, militant foreign policy.

Becker's analysis is on the mark: "satisfied with certain
conventional premises, [America] hastens on to the obvious
conclusion." All that said, it is nevertheless important to understand that the agricultural pressure for overseas empire
was ultimately pre-empted by urban leaders. The agricul-

businesspeople lost control of their own idea and pro-
am. The details of that story, an almost epic tale of the
battle for control of an idea, have been explored by many
historians.* But the gist of it is very simple: metropolitan
leaders recognized the necessity of expansion for the capitalist political economy—industrial and financial as well as agricultural—and deployed their more concentrated and efficient
power to define and control the new idiom of empire as a
way of life.

Their victory was not the result of a conspiracy. The concentration of power in the urban, industrial centers was the
key to their triumph. Agricultural businesspeople were individualistic, geographically diffused, and very busy at hard
labor most of the time. Urban capitalists were concentrated
and had time to develop and coordinate policy. Adam Smith
said it once and for all: the city has a structural advantage
over the country. Urban leaders took over an agricultural
idea, adapted it to their purposes, and put it into action.

No one knows the name of the first metropolitan capitalist
who recognized the validity of the agricultural argument for
overseas economic expansion. But we do know that John D.
Rockefeller of Standard Oil was busy, as early as the late
1870s, exporting kerosene to Asians in order to survive. "We
were forced to extend our markets and to seek for export
trade." Many, many industrialists soon learned that lesson.
Firms that made hardware—hammers and pliers—challenged
British manufacturers for the market in Australia, and An-

* An overview is offered in my *The Roots of the Modern American Empire* (New York:
Random House, 1969). But there is much more in E. P. Crapol, *America for Americans* (Westport, Conn.: Greenwood Press, 1973); W. LaFeber, *The New Empire* (Ithaca: Cornell University Press, 1963); M. Plesur *America's Outward Thrust* (DeKalb;
Northern Illinois University Press, 1971); D. M. Pletcher, *The Awkward Years* (Columbia: University of Missouri Press, 1962); H. B. Schonberger, *Transportation to
the Seaboard: The "Communications Revolution" and American Foreign Policy* (Westport,
Conn.: Greenwood Press, 1971); and T. E. Terrill, *The Tariff, Politics, and American
Foreign Policy 1874–1901* (Westport, Conn.: Greenwood Press, 1973).

drew Carnegie worked overtime to unload railroad iron anywhere in the world.

Rockefeller and Carnegie, even those who never made their kind of fortunes, were intellectuals: individuals who made it their business (*literally*) to make coherent, inclusive sense out of all the seemingly separate, unrelated facts that came across their desks every day. Hence it is very difficult, perhaps impossible, to decide who determined the outcome of the conflict between the agricultural and urban businessmen. Academic intellectuals, historians for example, like to think that the decision was determined by their own kind—thinkers removed from the sweat and swill of the marketplace.

And, make no mistake about it, they can make a strong case. Particularly if they are allowed to include the kind of politician who defines his constituency as the effective functioning of the *system* rather than the short-term prosperity and indifference of the citizens in his voting district. Such politicians may or may not be statesmen (whatever that means), but they do most certainly think very seriously about how to sustain empire as a way of life.

And precisely here is where the urban expansionists proved superior to their agricultural competitors. Watson, Simpson, Donnelly, and Lloyd were simply no match for William Henry Seward, James G. Blaine, William Henry Harrison, and William McKinley. Or naval strategists such as Stephen B. Luce or Alfred Thayer Mahan. Or religious and secular revivalists like Josiah Strong and John Fiske. Or ambitious aristocrats named Brooks Adams, Henry Cabot Lodge, and Theodore Roosevelt. And an academic like Frederick Jackson Turner who simply and boldly asserted that imperial expansion was the foundation of liberty, prosperity, and democracy. Even corporation intellectuals such as Charles A. Conant and J. P. Morgan.

Those were powerful and persuasive minds focused on the

explicit or implicit need to transform the idea and the tradition and the reality of continental empire into global empire. Their opponents, agricultural or urban, failed to devise a persuasive non-imperial alternative. One may doubt that even Karl Marx could have done so. Indeed, Marx would very probably have shrugged his shoulders (and ideology) and said only that socialism is *unimaginable*, let alone pragmatically possible, until capitalist empire has run its course.

And so it began to run its course. From Alaska to Midway to Samoa to Hawaii to China to Cuba to the Philippines and back to China. The continental empire was dead, long live the empire. But, recognized or not, the ghost of Lincoln wandered the seascape of the new imperial way of life. The problem perhaps transformed itself, but Lincoln would have understood it all. How does one use the evil of empire to sustain, extend, and guarantee the good of freedom, prosperity, and security? American history continued to be defined by the search for the answer to that question.

APPENDIX
American Interventionist Activity
(excluding declared wars) from 1829 to 1898.

1831–32   Falkland Islands. To investigate the capture of three American sealing vessels and to protect American interests.

1832   Sumatra—February 6 to 9. To punish natives of the town of Quallah Battoo for depredations on American shipping.

1833   Argentina—October 31 to November 15. A force was sent ashore at Buenos Aires to protect the interests of the United States and other countries during an insurrection.

1835–36   Peru—December 10, 1835 to January 24, 1836. Marines protected American interests in Callao and Lima during an attempted revolution.

1836   Mexico. General Gaines occupied Nacogdoches (Tex.), disputed territory, from July to December during the Texan war for independence, under order to cross the "imaginary boundary line" if an Indian outbreak threatened.

1838–39   Sumatra—December 24, 1838 to January 4, 1938. To punish natives of the towns of Quallah Battoo and Muckie (Mukki) for depredations on American shipping.

1840   Fiji Islands—July. To punish natives for attacking American exploring and surveying parties.

1841   Drummond Island, Kingsmill Group. To avenge the murder of a seaman by the natives.

1841   Samoa—February 24. To avenge the murder of a seaman on Upolu Island.

1843   Mexico. Commodore T. A. C. Jones in command of a squadron long cruising off California, occupied Monterey, Calif., on October 19, believing war had come. He discovered peace, withdrew, and saluted. A similar incident occurred a week later at San Diego.

1843   Africa—November 29 to December 16. Four United States vessels demonstrated and landed various parties (one of 200 marines and sailors) to discourage piracy and the slave trade along the Ivory Coast, etc., and to punish attacks by the natives on American seamen and shipping.

1844   Mexico. President Tyler deployed our forces to protect Texas against Mexico, pending Senate approval of a treaty of annexation (later rejected). He defended his action against a Senate resolution of inquiry. This was a demonstration of preparation.

1846–48   Mexico, the Mexican war. President Polk's occupation of disputed territory precipitated it.

1849   Smyrna. In July a naval force gained release of an American seized by Austrian officials.

1851   Turkey. After a massacre of foreigners (including Americans) at Jaffa in January, a demonstration by our Mediterranean Squadron was ordered along the Turkish (Levant) coast. Apparently no shots fired.

1851   Joahanna Island (east of Africa), August. To exact redress for the unlawful imprisonment of the captain of an American whaling brig.

1852–53   Argentina—February 3 to 12, 1852; September 17, 1852 to April (?), 1853. Marines were landed and maintained in Buenos Aires to protect American interests during a revolution.

1853   Nicaragua—March 11 to 13. To protect American lives and interests during political disturbances.

1853–54   Japan. The "opening of Japan" and the Perry expedition.

1853–54   Ryukyu and Bonin Islands. Commodore Perry on three visits before going to Japan and while waiting for a reply from Japan made a naval demonstration, landing marines twice, and secured a coaling concession from the ruler of Naha on Okinawa. He also demonstrated in the Bonin Islands. All to secure facilities for commerce.

1854   China—April 4 to June 15 or 17. To protect American interests in and near Shanghai during Chinese civil strife.

1854   Nicaragua—July 9 to 15. San Juan del Norte (Greytown) was destroyed to avenge an insult to the American Minister to Nicaragua.

1855   China—May 19 to 21. To protect American interests in Shanghai; August 3 to 5, to fight pirates near Hong Kong.

1855   Fiji Islands—September 12 to November 4. To seek reparations for depredations on Americans.

1855   Uruguay—November 25 to 29 or 30. United States and European naval forces landed to protect American interests during an attempted revolution in Montevideo.

1856   Panama, Republic of New Grenada—September 19 to 22. To protect American interests during an insurrection.

1856   China—October 22 to December 6. To protect American interests at Canton during hostilities between the British and the Chinese; and to avenge an unprovoked assault upon an unarmed boat displaying the United States flag.

1857   Nicaragua—April to May, November to December. To oppose William Walker's attempt to get control of the country. In May, Commander C. H. Davis of the U. S. Navy, with some marines, received Walker's surrender and protected his men from the retaliation of native allies who had been fighting Walker. In November and December of the same year United States vessels *Saratoga*, *Wabash*, and *Fulton* opposed another attempt of William Walker on Nicaragua. Commodore Hiram Paulding's act of landing marines and compelling the removal of Walker to the United States was tacitly disavowed by Secretary of State Lewis Cass, and Paulding was forced into retirement.

1858   Uruguay—January 2 to 27. Forces from two United States warships landed to protect American property during a revolution in Montevideo.

1858   Fiji Islands—October 6 to 16. To chastise the natives for the murder of two American citizens.

1858–59 Turkey. Display of naval force along the Levant at the request of the Secretary of State after massacre of Americans at Jaffa and mistreatment elsewhere "to remind the authorities [of Turkey] . . . of the power of the United States."

1858   Paraguay. Congress authorized a naval squadron to seek redress for an attack on a naval vessel in the Parana River duriಸg 1855. Apologies were made after a large display of force.

1858   Mexico. Two hundred United States soldiers crossed the Rio Grande in pursuit of the Mexican bandit Cortina.

1858   China—July 31 to August 2. For the protection of American interests in Shanghai.

1860   Angola, Portuguese West Africa—March 1. To protect American lives and property at Kissembo when the natives became troublesome.

1860   Colombia, Bay of Panama—September 27 to October 8. To protect American interests during a revolution.

1863   Japan—July 16. To redress an insult to the American flag—firing on an American vessel—at Shimonoseki.

1864   Japan—July 14 to August 3, approximately. To protect the United States Minister to Japan when he visited Yedo to negotiate concerning some American claims against Japan, and to make his negotiations easier by impressing the Japanese with American power.

1864   Japan—September 4 to 14—Strait of Shimonoseki. To compel Japan and the Prince of Nagato in particular to permit the Strait to be used by foreign shipping in accordance with treaties already signed.

1865   Panama—March 9 and 10. To protect the lives and property of American residents during a revolution.

1866   Mexico. To protect American residents. General Sedgwick and 100 men in November obtained surrender of Matamoras. After three days he was ordered by our U.S. government to withdraw. His act was repudiated by the President.

1866　China—June 20 to July 7. To punish an assault on the American consul at Newchwang; July 14, for consultation with authorities on shore; August 9, at Shanghai, to help extinguish a serious fire in the city.

1867　Island of Formosa—June 13. To punish a horde of savages who were alleged to have murdered the crew of a wrecked American vessel.

1868　Japan (Osaka, Hiogo, Nagasaki, Yokohama, and Negata)—mainly February 4 to 8, April 4 to May 12, June 12 and 13. To protect American interests during the civil war in Japan over the abolition of the Shogunate and the restoration of the Mikado.

1868　Uruguay—February 7 and 8, 19 and 26. To protect foreign residents and the customhouse during an insurrection at Montevideo.

1868　Colombia—April 7—at Aspinwall. To protect passengers and treasure in transit during the absence of local police or troops on the occasion of the death of the President of Colombia.

1870　Mexico—June 17 and 18. To destroy the pirate ship *Forward*, which had been run aground about forty miles up the Rio Tecapan.

1870　Hawaiian Islands—September 21. To place the American flag at half mast upon the death of Queen Kalama, when the American consul at Honolulu would not assume responsibility for so doing.

1871　Korea—June 10 to 12. To punish natives for depredations on Americans, particularly for murdering the crew of the *General Sherman* and burning the schooner, and for later firing on other American small boats taking soundings up the Saico River.

1873　Colombia (Bay of Panama)—May 7 to 22, September 23 to October 9. To protect American interests during hostilities over possession of the government of the State of Panama.

1873   Mexico—United States troops crossed the Mexican border repeatedly in pursuit of cattle- and other thieves. There were some reciprocal pursuits by Mexican troops into our border territory. The cases were invasions only technically, if that, although Mexico protested constantly. Notable cases were at Remolina in May 1873 and at Las Cuevas in 1975. *Washington orders often supported these excursions. Agreements between Mexico and the United States, the first in* 1882, finally legitimized such raids. They continued intermittently, with minor disputes, until 1896.

1874   Hawaiian Islands—February 12 to 20. To preserve order and protect American lives and interests during the inauguration of a new king.

1876   Mexico—May 18. To police the town of Matamoros temporarily while it was without other government.

1882   Egypt—July 14 to 18. To protect American interests during warfare between British and Egyptians and looting by Arabs of the city of Alexandria.

1885   Panama (Colon)—January 18 and 19. To guard the valuables in transit over the Panama Railroad, and the safes and vaults of the company during revolutionary activity. In March, April, and May in the cities of Colon and Panama, to re-establish freedom of transit during revolutionary activity.

1888   Korea—June. To protect American residents in Seoul during unsettled political conditions, when outbreak of the populace was expected.

1888–89 Samoa—November 14, 1888 to March 20, 1889. To protect American citizens and the consulate during a native civil war.

1888   Haiti—December 20. To persuade the Haitian government to give up an American steamer which had been seized on the charge of breach of blockade.

1889   Hawaiian Islands—July 30 and 31. To protect American interests at Honolulu during a revolution.

1890   Argentina. A naval party landed to protect the United States consulate and legation in Buenos Aires.

1891   Haiti. To protect American lives and property on Navessa Island when Negro laborers got out of control.

1891   Bering Sea—July 2 to October 5. To stop seal poaching.

1891   Chile—August 28 to 30. To protect the American consulate and the women and children who had taken refuge in it during a revolution in Valparaiso.

1893   Hawaii—January 16 to April 1 Ostensibly to protect American lives and property; actually to promote a provisional government under Sanford B. Dole. This action was disavowed by the United States.

1894   Brazil—January. To protect American commerce and shipping at Rio de Janeiro during a Brazilian civil war. No landing was attempted but there was a display of naval force.

1894   Nicaragua—July 6 to August 7. To protect American interests at Bluefields following a revolution.

1894–96   Korea—July 24, 1894 to April 3, 1896. To protect American lives and interests at Seoul during and following the Sino-Japanese war. A guard of marines was kept at the American legation most of the time until April 1896.

1894–95   China. Marines were stationed at Tientsin and penetrated to Peking for protection purposes during the Sino-Japanese war.

1894–95 China. Naval vessel beached and used as a fort at Newchwang for protection of American nationals.

1895 Colombia—March 8 to 9. To protect American interests during an attack on the town of Bocas del Toro by a bandit chieftain.

1896 Nicaragua—May 2 to 4. To protect American interests in Corinto during political unrest.

CHAPTER SIX

A Benevolent and Progressive Policeman: The Self-Image of Global Empire

[Americans are] for ever brooding over advantages they do not possess . . . with the bootless chase of that complete felicity which is for ever on the wing.

ALEXIS DE TOCQUEVILLE,
Democracy in America, 1835

Chronic wrongdoing, or an impotence which results in a general loosening of the ties of civilized society, may. . . . in the Western Hemisphere . . . force the United States, however reluctantly . . . to the exercise of an international police power.

PRESIDENT THEODORE ROOSEVELT, 1904

The diplomacy of the present administration . . . is an effort frankly directed to the increase of American trade . . . [As a part of our] international philanthropy.

PRESIDENT WILLIAM HOWARD TAFT, 1912

The program of the world's peace, therefore, is our program . . . the only possible program.

PRESIDENT WOODROW WILSON, 1918

THE crusading, punitive, and imperial war against Spain (1898–99), generated by forces that emerged during the previous two generations, posed intellectual, moral, and strategic problems that Americans failed to resolve during the ensuing century. That inability to integrate profit and reform with security and purity was not surprising. Not even Walt Whitman had been able to sanitize the assault on Mexico, and Lincoln proved incapable of exorcising the ghost of self-determination that hovered over all the battlefields of the War Between the States. The Wilsons and the Roosevelts proved no more successful.

The combination of specific and general pressures which produced the gratuitous attack on Spain, and the subsequent assertion of formal control over Hawaii, Cuba, and the Philippines, created a national sense of euphoria that temporarily masked a most serious problem. True, the citizens and the government of the United States had steadily expanded their activities, influence, power, and dreams beyond continental North America during the 19th century. But the dramatic acceleration and intensification of that imperial outreach made it necessary to develop an appropriate ideology, to coordinate and institutionalize the continental and overseas parts of the imperial political economy, and to devise a military strategy that would preserve and extend the empire without wasting its psychic or cultural or economic substance.

The ensuing debate and activities, interacting with each other, gradually produced an image among Americans of the United States as a benevolent, progressive policeman. It was a satisfying self-portrait, given extra depth and color by the domestic reforms of the era. We would improve the world just as we perfected ourselves. But in truth the benevolence abroad was like the help at home: it went to a minority of the population. And the policeman became ever more energetic in whacking the skulls of strikers and blacks at home, as well as thumping feisty natives abroad. Americans increasingly discounted or ignored the costs and consequences of empire. They began to ignore the possibility that empire as a way of life was not the cultural version of a perpetual-motion machine.

Some Americans have always understood that a sense of history involves comprehending and coming to terms with the consequences of one's actions. But our fundamental, persistent way of life is predicated upon a charming but ruthless faith in infinite progress fueled by endless growth. Hence empire as a way of life projected beyond the continent to the world. Growth is the key to individual liberty and progress. The substance of growth is empire. Thus empire is benevolent. Hence the policeman who guarantees the growth of the law and order that is necessary to progress is undeniably benevolent.

That self-legitimizing dynamism was rooted in Jeffersonian universalism, was implicit in the Monroe Doctrine, became blatant in the spirit (and practice) of Manifest Destiny, and was carried forward less dramatically by the expansion of American economic activities beyond the continent and the related demands for government assistance and protection. Thus the intellectual problem is defined less as a need to reconstruct the daily interaction of those elements during the decade between 1893 and 1903 than by the challenge to understand how it was all of a piece—the continued fleeing forward of a culture that lacked any other tradition or strategy for dealing with its inherent or occasional problems.* Or, to put it another way, the central question is how the faith and practice of individualism based upon expansion became dependence upon the imperial police power of the ever more awesome state.

In approaching this issue, it is useful to understand the role that Adam Smith assigned to such state power in his grand theory of marketplace capitalism. Long before he wrote *The Wealth of Nations*, Smith lectured at length on the interrelationship of *Justice, Police, Revenue, and Arms*. And, in his reflections in *Moral and Political Philosophy*, he was unequivocal: "The peace and order of society is of more importance than even the relief of the miserable." That judgment was born less of callousness than of logic. For in arguing that laissez-faire would produce ever more wealth, Smith had to insist upon the law and order required to provide the framework for the magic of individual liberty and acquisitiveness to generate such growth.

He made all that explicit in *The Wealth of Nations*. The state had "the duty of protecting, as far as possible, every member

---

*This is not to discount the importance of detailed reconstruction and analysis. Those activities provide the foundation for any effort to deal with cultural phenomena. I see no reason to undertake that work here because it has already been done by many resourceful, imaginative, and thoughtful scholars. In the case of the Spanish-American War and its immediate consequences, for example, begin by consulting these studies: E. P. Crapol, *America for Americans* (Westport, Conn.: Greenwood Press, 1973); W. LaFeber, *The New Empire* (Ithaca: Cornell University Press, 1963); T. J. McCormick, *China Market* (Chicago: Quadrangle, 1967); B. I. Kaufman, *Efficiency and Expansion* (Westport, Conn.: Greenwood Press, 1974); and J. Israel, *Progressivism and the Open Door* (Pittsburgh: University of Pittsburgh Press, 1971).

of the society from the injustice or oppression of every other member of it, or the duty of establishing an exact administration of justice." He then added that such police power first of all involved protecting the marketplace conception of reality from the consequences of the "great inequality" produced by the marketplace—the rich from the poor—and more generally enforcing that "certain subordination" essential to civil government. Given Smith's insistence upon the expansion of the marketplace to generate and underwrite individual freedom and the general welfare, there is no wonder that he stressed "the exact administration." *But the exact administration of justice on a global scale demanded a global empire.*

Within that context, it is next useful to review the various styles of police activity. There are several ways to describe those different idioms, but the most helpful is based on these terms: the watchman, the legalistic, and the service. The first concentrates on keeping the peace. The second functions on the assumption that there is a single standard of conduct. The third honors the values and priorities of its particular community. As we shall see, the American image of itself as a policeman included, even synthesized, all those ideas.

One does not need to be able to twist clouds into pretzels to imagine how those three criteria could merge and define one all-encompassing purpose: keeping the peace as dictated by one community's definition of the single standard of conduct. For the moment, however, let us explore the way in which the concepts of benevolence, progressive, and policeman are inherently double-edged. Like all root words, those terms are in truth metaphors which, through the actions taken in their names, acquire multiple meanings. And those in turn subvert their explicit substance. The word comes to mean something else, not merely to those who are subjected to the word, but to those who use the word.

We can observe how this process proceeds by listing below the key word the various contents that it absorbs and comes to mean. On the left the basic meaning, and on the right (without any direct lineal equation) the sense acquired by the nature and the consequences of the action. Note particularly how the words begin to merge into one image.

BENEVOLENT

helpfulness	bestow a benediction
innocence	grant a favor
charity	patronize
brotherliness	put one under an obligation
generosity	make better, improve
tolerance	reform
disinterested	go slumming
steward	mother

PROGRESSIVE

dynamic	aggressive
enterprise	overtake
prosperity	purgation
reform	irreversible
modernize	outstrip
improve	put right
uplift	irresistible
purify	never look back

POLICEMAN

order	regulate
systematic	keep one's place
discipline	surveillance
secure	patronize
quarantine, protect	hegemonic
warden	authoritarian
steward	paternalism
benevolent	lord-it-over

So alerted, so informed, let us now explore how the war against Spain transformed such apparently abstract exercises into the substance of the new American Empire.

II

The American interest in Cuba had an ancient, even royal, history. The Elizabethans hankered after Cuba, for example, as a base for their piracy against the Spanish and for its indigenous wealth. Two centuries later, northern as well as southern colonials were no less acquisitive. Franklin placed Cuba high on his list of priorities in 1761, and Jefferson pushed that acquisitiveness into the 19th century. By the beginning of the 1840s, expansionists of all persuasions were regularly linking Cuba the "ripe pear" with Hawaii the "luscious fruit." And in subsequent years both islands became symbols for prosperous outposts of missionary regeneration and erotic bastions of American security and spheres of influence.

The argument that Cuba needed to be controlled, if not literally occupied, to protect the southern approach to the vast Mississippi Valley Basin (undeniably the primary strategic objective of any enemy concerned to acquire the wealth of the continental American Empire) was defensible, though not unchallengeable, as purely military logic. As in considering all such arguments, however, that syllogism must be evaluated on the basis of the intention, as well as the capability, of the ostensible enemies. Otherwise the definition of security becomes control of the world, as with Jefferson's doctrine that the only way to avoid trouble with neighbors is to acquire or dominate them—a conception of security that has little to do with strategy and much to do with paranoid acquisitiveness.

All that said, the legitimate concern about Cuba was heightened by the North's difficulties in blockading the

Confederacy, by the French effort between 1863 and 1867 to establish a dynasty in Mexico, and by the subsequent revival of the American effort to control any isthmian canal between the Atlantic and the Pacific. In the broader sense, however, the imperial excitement about the French and the British was kindled by ideological, psychological, and economic concerns that were less provoked from abroad than ignited at home. What we Americans wanted, or had decided that we needed for our domestic welfare, became ennobled as a strategic necessity. Security in the elementary sense was increasingly lost in the clouds of righteous and benevolent desire.

The grapeshot rhetoric about America as the exemplar, advocate, and protector of self-determination and progress in the western hemisphere was once again loaded into the intellectual cannons and fired off against the French and the British. And still another time Washington sent troops to the Mexican border. It was all a bit repetitive. No wonder, then, that when the Cubans erupted in 1868 in what became a decade of bloody rebellion and revolution, the Americans were delighted to include the Spanish in the expanding denunciation of European machinations against liberty and profit and progress.

The Spanish managed to defeat that uprising, but they failed to use the victory to create a new and viable relationship with the Cubans. When those citizens again revolted in 1895, moreover, the traditional American concern about the island was intensified by five dynamic and mutually reinforcing developments of the intervening years. The first was the steady expansion of American economic activity beyond the continent (and even the hemisphere). Individuals and companies were centrally involved in the growth of the industrial as well as the agricultural part of the economy, and hence they engaged the entire system. The export statistics were not enormous when compared, say, with those for the British Empire; but they were significant for the people involved and, even more importantly, they were increasingly perceived by leaders as well as interested advocates as defining the future health of the American political economy.

Second, America had recovered emotionally and ideologically from the exhaustion of the Civil War. As if a phoenix, it burst forth in evangelical energy and enthusiasm. The glowing feathers, secular as well as religious, fluttered about in foreign as well as in domestic affairs. The revived urge to save and reform, if not transform, the world appeared among businessmen, church people, politicians, intellectuals, and even naval officers. Reform at home justified empire abroad.

Third, another major marketplace crisis created fears that the capitalist political economy might collapse and spawn socialism or anarchy—thereby subverting the American mission to extend the area of freedom. The massive domestic depression triggered by the Panic of 1893 was quickly related, moreover, to the world marketplace. That occurred in two ways: through an intensified emphasis upon foreign markets to end the depression; and a related concern that Japan and the major European powers were going to partition China—the one great remaining segment of the global marketplace—among themselves. America was entering into the argument among the rich about how to control the poor.

Fourth, the marketplace crisis (in both its domestic and foreign aspects) dramatized and intensified the cultural crisis created by the shift from an agrarian-commercial political economy to an industrial-financial system. The agriculturalists—the country—were losing their formerly superior *structural* power to the manufacturers and the bankers—the city or metropolis. The farmers and their allies (in the crossroads but also in the communication cities) understood the change and all that it portended for their social and intellectual value system, economic priorities, and political agenda. The country, which had built the city, was losing power to the city.

Finally, all those developments encouraged—indeed, demanded—people to think about the marketplace as an integrated system requiring centralized direction rather than as a collection of random individuals whose self-interested activities magically produced the general welfare. Even those who clung to the pure Smithian doctrine of the marketplace began to agitate for more vigorous action by the government to expand the marketplace to preserve America's uniqueness. They wanted more expansion abroad, more empire, to preserve individualist freedom at home.

The interaction of those elements poses a difficult problem of analysis. It can be dealt with effectively, however, through a process known as factoring-out. That odd-man-out intellectual strategy involves deciding which element is crucial to the known outcome. If we abstract that component, cancel it out, then there will be no war against Spain and no related conception of America as a benevolent, progressive policeman.

In my judgment, the essential ingredient was the massive depression. It dramatized and intensified the urban-rural conflict; it accelerated and focused the search for new markets on Cuba and China; it centered the evangelical revival—secular as well as religious—upon the rich as well as the poor. It also infused all those matters with either-or emotions, demanding that a choice be made; and all in all it gave the people who thought of the marketplace as a system a psychological and intellectual and practical advantage over those who merely agitated for their special interest or truth.

Given the depression of the 1890s, it was impossible to deal calmly or abstractly with the revolutionary turmoil in Cuba and the situation in Asia. The minority which sought to do so, regardless of whether they were trying to revive the principle of self-determination or counting on the quiet triumph of American economic expansion (or both), was simply outmaneuvered and overpowered by those who de-

manded vigorous and systematic action on both fronts—
Cuba and China—as an integrated solution to interrelated
problems of the American Empire.

Not at all surprisingly, albeit sadly and ironically, many of
those who sought more democracy at home (such as the reforming farmers and workers) supplied ideological and economic and political, and even social and intellectual, pressures
that pushed the systematic imperialists along to victory. The
farmers, for example, demanded freedom and prosperity for
themselves through the expansion of markets; but that was
precisely the program advocated by their adversaries in the
city. And the farmers vented the kind of strident rhetoric
about liberty abroad that encouraged an ideology of intervention that enabled those who wanted less liberty at home to
justify themselves in the name of an empire abroad that had
no primary concern for the welfare or the freedom of the foreigners.

Such ideological, emotional, intellectual, and political turmoil created increasing uncertainty and fear about the survival of the system. In particular, the marketplace failure so
exacerbated the cultural crisis that Cuba became the focus of
the tensions and conflicts which seemed to be tearing the
country apart. Thus the crucial question became how, and
where, and for what purposes, to use force.

The question was *how*, that is to say, not *whether*, to
sustain empire as a way of life. In the beginning, say from
1895 well into 1896, most Americans focused their attention
on Cuba and favored economic intervention to help the revolutionaries. Then they approved military assistance perhaps
culminating in a short expedition to finish the job of freeing
the island. But the escalation of the domestic and cultural
crises pushed increasing numbers of people—populist but
also conservative—to favor a war against Spain. Along the
way, ever more leaders came to think of Cuba in terms of
China—meaning that freeing Cuba could lead to a beachhead

in the Philippines (also owned by Spain) for access to Asia. All those pressures, economic, political, and visionary, prompted President Grover Cleveland to ask the navy for a war plan.

The men in gold and blue responded with an imperial strategy that linked Cuba with the Philippines. For many years, historians and other scholars discounted both the significance and the influence of the navy during the decades after the Civil War. That analysis had some validity, particularly in comparing the size and quality of various European battle fleets. But that approach is seriously misleading because it neglects what the navy was actually doing with the ships that it kept at sea, the steady momentum of modernization after 1881, the expanding intellectual and political influence of leaders like Benjamin F. Tracy and Alfred T. Mahan, and the support for the navy generated by leaders of the urban, industrial part of the political economy. For that matter, even the romance with the sea carried on by reformist politicians from the Middle West. Whatever the glorious memories of the victories of Grant and Sherman, and despite the army's role in destroying the Indians of the West, the navy had by 1885 reasserted itself as the premier military service.

It had earned that place through its performance at sea, moreover, as well as ashore. Consider, for example, the sustained overseas cruising records of the various fleets on station outside the waters of North America and Europe. Stephen S. Roberts's excellent study of that activity tells us that such ships made 5,980 port calls between 1869 and 1897.* The performance of the Asiatic Squadron is partially illuminating in the context of the navy's plan for war against Spain. Not only did the navy maintain a sustained presence

---

*S. S. Roberts, "An Indicator of Informal Empire: Patterns of U.S. Navy Cruising on Overseas Stations, 1869–1897." Available from the author at the Center for Naval Analysis, Alexandria, Virginia.

in China, Japan, and Korea; but also, whatever the vicissitudes of overall strength, that station was not allowed to decline. And the Pacific Squadron, responsible for an enormous area, had the largest number of ships and deployed them throughout the islands on a regular basis. The navy concentrated such activity at the major commercial and political centers. As Roberts observes: American naval policy "was to ensure law and order and secure economic access through the local power structure if at all possible, while preventing European powers . . . from obtaining privileges that would exclude Americans."

Given that pattern of action, underscored as it was by Mahan's grand vision of America astride the oceans of the world, it is not surprising that the navy offered President Cleveland an imperial rather than a local strategy. The proposal to destroy Spanish power in the Philippines as an integral part of resolving the Cuban issue meant at the least that the United States would acquire a base of operations on China's doorstep, and notified other powers that America would not passively accept being excluded from that part of the global marketplace. Cleveland accepted the plan, as did President William McKinley.

The navy could have offered a far less grandiose strategy based upon the classic maneuver of crossing the line of enemy ships. Indeed, the circumstances favored such a proposal. That would have called for Commodore George Dewey's Asiatic Squadron to do nothing more than steam back and forth across the entrance to Manila harbor. If the Spanish fleet emerged to run for Cuba, it could easily be turned back or sunk. Americans enjoyed the same kind of advantage in the Cuban situation, for any trans-Atlantic reinforcements would arrive in the same inferior position.

It is theoretically possible, but pragmatically highly improbable, that McKinley, his advisers, and other leaders failed to comprehend either those options or the consequences of the navy's recommendation. Thus we can fairly conclude that they had decided, if force was required, that they would deploy it across the board to achieve a quick and global victory. That choice was not made by a conspiracy among closet imperialists. It was the result of the dynamic interaction of the depression, the cultural crisis, the ferment in Asia, and the emotional and pragmatic commitment to the military strategy of annihilation that Lincoln had embraced during the Civil War.

And so empire as a way of life was reintegrated and projected out across the globe. Revolutionaries in Cuba who wanted true independence were ignored, isolated, or simply overpowered. Their compatriots in the Philippines were hunted down and shot, subjected to water torture, or killed in other ways—and likewise defeated. But all that annihilation abroad posed the same problems that it had earlier created at home. The First Americans had been destroyed as cultural entities without bringing the survivors into the marketplace society heralded as superior to tribal society. And neither the white nor black members of the Confederacy had been integrated as equal members of the American Empire for Liberty. The process of expanding the area of freedom to the world produced similar consequences.

III

The essence of American culture had come to have less to do with the transformation of avowed intentions and ideals into institutional arrangements, and the related exploration and cultivation of those ideals, than with the avoidance of such human and humane challenges through the pursuit of growth. The culture had been unable, after almost 300 years, to develop any conception of success—or fulfillment—except the idiom of the endless chase itself. It was all a footnote to Madison: "extend the sphere." Americans thought, talked, and devised policy for the glories of the future whatever the troubles, limitations, and failures of the present. They appeared constitutionally unable to settle for *developing* and *enriching* their existing empire. They defined development and enrichment as ever more growth—ever more empire.

Various Americans, as well as foreigners, had recognized and commented upon the pattern long before the imperial war against Spain. Such "restless[ness] in the midst of abundance" was nothing new in *individuals*, noted Alexis de Tocqueville in 1835: "the novelty is to see a whole people furnish an exemplification of it." Americans are "for ever brooding over advantages they do not possess," and are obsessed "with the bootless chase of that complete felicity which is for ever on the wing." Even those Americans who tried to counter such judgments could offer little more than the hope—or belief—that such childish behavior would end as the United States reached maturity. Others, such as Henry W. Bellows, an influential northerner who founded Antioch College, were less confident. As long as Americans defined freedom and individualism in marketplace terms, they would be possessed by an "anxious spirit of gain" that manifested itself in seeking an objective "which in its very nature is unobtainable—the perpetual improvement of the outward condition."

There are countless expressions of that American restlessness in the name of liberty, mission, and material progress. But Thomas H. Norton, an American consular officer in the Middle East, said it as well as any of the more famous spokesmen of imperialism. He defended the vigor, even aggressiveness, of religious and secular missionaries penetrating an Islamic culture in this way: "In a thousand ways they are raising the standard of morality, of intelligence, of education. . . . Directly or indirectly every phase of their work is rapidly paving the way for American commerce. . . . I know of no import better adapted to secure the future commercial supremacy of the United States." And that, of course, was the key to the progress of "this land of such wonderful potential possibilities." The world would become better as it aped the American example.

That bootless chase of complete felicity was accelerated and extended, and ultimately rationalized, by the ruthless and unconditional defeat of the Spanish. The Spanish gave over as Lee gave over to Grant. The Americans would decide the future of Cuba and the Philippines. "There was no other outcome or outlook," explained one euphoric advocate—or was it acolyte—of empire. It was all an answer to "divine commands," echoed another. "The Republic could not retreat if it would; whatever its destiny, it must proceed." It was "our duty to the world as one of its civilizing powers." Perhaps the spirit of it all was best expressed this way: "It is the law of nature, the human longing for the change and for the new, the never latent and irresistible force of progress. . . . The western course of the 'star of empire' is one of its most noted manifestations." While many tied Nature and Progress to the chariot of marketplace capitalism, none did it better than Brooks Adams. "It is in vain," he observed, that men talk of alternatives. "Nature is omnipotent; and nations must float with the tide. Whither the exchanges flow, they must follow."

The process of combining and formulating all those elements of American imperialism into a coherent global strategy that could be implemented as policy was guided by several traditional axioms. Various individuals and groups emphasized different themes, and disagreed about tactical matters. Those arguments produced scintillating rhetoric; but the consequential dialogue, while less effervescent, concerned the *means not the whether* of empire.

A small group of people of all colors and both sexes did oppose the new imperial system. If they had developed and agreed upon a shared alternative, they just might have changed the terms of the discussion about the character of

American culture. But they quickly divided according to their respective recipes for ultimate felicity: in the main a division between those who advocated capitalism in one continent (or hemisphere) and others who mimicked global capitalism in the name of international socialism. Each group now and again exerted some influence on policy. Yet, arguing among and between themselves, they dissipated their potential clout and so failed to redefine the dialogue as a debate about how to realize American ideals in a non-imperial context. Thus the primary issue remained one of structuring an empire in the name of freedom and welfare.

Confronting that problem, Americans in general, and their leaders in particular, relied upon six cultural fundamentals in devising their response. First, the Smithian political economy predicated upon equal access to, and treatment in, the capitalist marketplace for all competitors produced the greatest good for the greatest number. Second, political, social, and intellectual freedoms were dependent upon that economic system. Economic freedom was the foundation of all freedom. Third, for that reason, as well as because of its own inherent logic, the system had at all costs to be maintained through expansion. Growth was the key to economic welfare and hence to all other good things. Fourth, the American example provided the ultimate proof of those propositions and was therefore the model for humankind's progress.

Fifth, the Monroe Doctrine offered the model for the policy appropriate to that golden future by providing traditionally successful rules for the global competition. Hands Off for marketplace competition to produce freedom and welfare. Sixth, the debate about which kind of military force would sustain and expand such an empire was decided in favor of the navy. It was at once imperially efficient and domestically clean—meaning that it could deliver fire power abroad without threatening the domestic political process.

All those beliefs and concerns, objectives and intentions,

were perfectly expressed—implicitly and explicitly—in the major messages that Secretary of State John Hay dispatched to the world across the turn of the century. The immediate context was defined by the situation in China, but they were statements of principle that were sooner rather than later applied to the world at large. For good reason, they have come to be known as the Open Door Notes: Hay was concerned to clear the way for American power to penetrate and dominate the global marketplace.

Those marvelous documents, two classic essays and a laconic footnote, bespoke a collective genius.* For, while they announced an imperial strategy of great power and consequence, they could also be cited as evidence of America's bedrock anti-imperialism. Hay's objective was to open the way for the endless expansion of the American frontier in the name of self-determination, progress, and peace. His psychological strategy was similar to the one employed by President McKinley in dealing with Spain over Cuba. In that instance, pointing to the domestic American unrest generated by that revolution, McKinley announced that Spain's failure to cope with the upheaval was responsible for the turmoil in the United States. Thus if Spain could not control Cuba, America would exercise its right to intervene to preserve its own political tranquility. Or, as Alexis de Tocqueville phrased it, "that complete felicity." For his part, Hay maneuvered other powers into an acceptance of, and acquiescence in, American principles and thus placed them on the defensive.

The Secretary's first objective was to reserve "perfect equality of treatment" for American "commerce and navigation" within any European or Japanese sphere of interest. The second was to make it clear that "commerce" included

---

* Circular notes to all powers on September 6, 1899, and July 3, 1900; followed by a dispatch to Germany of October 29, 1900.

financial operations. The third was to "bring about permanent safety and peace to China, preserve Chinese territorial and administrative entity . . . and safeguard for the world the principle of equal and impartial trade with all parts of the Chinese Empire." The final objective, whose implications are sometimes overlooked, involved "affording all possible protection everywhere in China to American life and property . . . in guarding and protecting all legitimate American interests, and . . . aiding to prevent a spread of the disorders to the other provinces of the Empire and a recurrence of such disasters."

In sum, Hay's policy was designed to establish principles, or rules of the game, which Americans considered essential for the immediate and long-range effectiveness of the expansion of their political economy. Those principles inherently and explicitly concerned the behavior of Chinese and other poor indigenous peoples as well as the actions of rival rich competitors in Europe and elsewhere. It equated such marketplace principles with freedom, liberty, and progress in all other areas of life. And it committed the United States to deploy its power in behalf of those principles.

Those who question such an imperial reading of Hay's policy often point out that the United States never embarked upon a program of acquiring colonies, or even spheres of influence, in the classic European way of empire. The map of the world has never been splashed with a color keyed to the continental United States in the way that it has been washed with the hues used for Great Britain, France, or Germany. The argument is formally correct and yet seriously misleading. On the one hand, American policy-makers never undertook to create that kind of an empire. On the other hand, a map colored to show primary or major economic, political, and military *power and influence* would reveal the United States as a global empire.

Such critics also insist that the deployment of American

power was progressive, benevolent, helped to secure the general peace, and extended freedom and welfare to many peoples of the world. But that is to admit the reality of the empire and shift the discussion to the question of how much benefit it produced for whom at what costs and consequences—the very subject of this essay. It is first necessary, however, to clarify the nature and operation of the empire.

It is illuminating in this connection to personalize the development of the empire between 1900 and 1920 around Theodore Roosevelt, William Howard Taft, and Woodrow Wilson. Let us use that perspective, keeping in mind that each of those men was responding to various groups (and even other individuals), as well as to the dynamic demands and needs of the economy. Thus Roosevelt's Big Stick can be seen as the embodiment of the theme of America as the policeman, Taft's emphasis on Dollar Diplomacy as the symbol of economic expansion, and Wilson's concern To Save the World for Democracy as the epitome of benevolent police action in the name of progress, freedom, and welfare.

However one explains Roosevelt's passion for law and order, and especially order, there is no doubt about his conception of America as a global policeman. Before he became President, for example, he justified and advocated such action in the name of civilization. "Barbarism" and other less dramatic kinds of misconduct must be disciplined in the name of true liberty—to free such societies and peoples "from their chains." Then in his annual messages to the Congress in 1904 and 1905, his most famous public statements of the principle, he applied it directly to the western hemisphere. Denying any land hunger or other motives for aggrandizement, but not the racial and cultural prejudices inherent in the concept, Roosevelt defined the proposition in this fashion.

"All that this country desires is that the other republics on this continent shall be happy and prosperous; and they cannot be happy and prosperous unless they maintain order within their boundaries and behave with a just regard for their obligations toward outsiders." Thus "chronic wrongdoing, or an impotence which results in a general loosening of the ties of civilized society, may . . . in the Western Hemisphere . . . force the United States, however reluctantly, . . . to the exercise of an international police power."

Roosevelt did *not* restrict that police power to Latin America, noting explicitly that America's efforts "to secure the open door in China" were part of the same effort to protect and extend "the interest of humanity at large." During the same years, moreover, he made it clear that his idea of America as an international policeman included action involving other rich and ostensibly civilized powers. During his intervention in the Russo-Japanese War, and in the scramble between France, Germany, and Britain for control of Morocco, the President left no doubt that he considered it necessary to maintain order within the rich neighborhoods as well as in the poor slums—as well as controlling the broader conflict between the rich and the poor. In a most consequential way, Roosevelt was defining America as the watchman (and enforcer) who acted on the basis of projecting its community values (and practices) as the single standard for the world.

As for enforcement, the President stressed the navy. He secured Congressional authorization for a total of 14 first-class battleships, 4 cruisers, and 17 other vessels; vigorously supported improvements in gunnery and other training; and sent the impressive results on a clearly imperial cruise around the world. But he did not neglect the army, giving Secretary of War Elihu Root firm backing to strengthen that arm of the police power by creating a War College and a General Staff Corps. Roosevelt made it clear to Root in a personal letter that it was all of a piece: "If we are willing to let Germany or England act as the policeman of the Caribbean, then we can afford not to intervene when gross wrongdoing occurs. But if we intend to say 'Hands Off' to the powers of Europe, then sooner or later we must keep order ourselves."

In comparison, President Taft's rhetoric and actions revealed a marketplace orientation. While Roosevelt approached control of the Panama Canal from the viewpoint of policing the flow of imperial traffic, Taft put it this way: "we own the canal"; after all, "it was our money that built it." In a similar vein, he sought ever closer economic ties with Canada in order to reduce that country to "only an adjunct of the United States." And hence his general concern with "the malady of revolutions" that produced "financial collapse."

Beyond those particulars, he analyzed the American situation in terms of the change in the political economy. The long years of acquiring and developing the domestic, continental empire were over: the United States had now "accumulated a surplus of capital beyond the requirements of internal development." Hence "our surplus energy is beginning to look beyond our own borders, throughout the world, to find opportunity for the profitable use of our surplus capital, foreign markets for our manufactures, foreign mines to be developed, foreign bridges and railroads and public works to be built, foreign rivers to be turned into electric power and light. . . ."

"Immediately before us, at exactly the right time, just as we are ready for it, great opportunities" are available. Other rich nations "are already in the field," but the openings are so great that America need not fear for its ultimate victory "in the race for the grand total." After all, the United States "is strenuous, intense, utilitarian," while Latin Americans and other such peoples are "polite, refined, cultivated, fond of literature and of expression and of the graces and charms of life." It will be no contest. Then came the marketplace advice: learn the markets and the language, provide the credit, and invest capital "as a means of creating and enlarging trade."

Taft summarized it this way: "The diplomacy of the present administration has sought to respond to modern ideas of commercial intercourse. This policy has been characterized as substituting dollars for bullets. . . . It is an effort frankly directed to the increase of American trade. . . . If this Government is really to preserve to the American people that free opportunity in foreign markets which will soon be indispensable to our prosperity, even greater efforts must be made." It was all a matter of "international philanthropy."

And so to Woodrow Wilson. His great admirers, beginning with himself, have sought to discount or even deny his understanding of the capitalist imperative to expand the marketplace, and his enjoyment in exercising police power in order to emphasize his benevolent progressivism. He simply wanted to do good for himself and his country by doing good for others. He can only be understood as a missionary. That is a disarming, even winsome, portrait. But let us probe that image. Begin with Wilson's benevolence, helpfulness, innocence, charity, tolerance, and stewardship. That leads us to his propensity to patronize, reform in his own image, go slumming, and to mother. Think of that list of words presented earlier in this chapter.

If we start with reform and go on to modernize, prosperity, improve, uplift, then we come out with purify, put right, purgation, overtake, and never look back. Finally, we find stewards as policemen, which leads us backwards and forwards to benevolence, surveillance, reform, paternalism, and systematic discipline in the name of progress as defined by the United States.

In order to put Wilson into perspective, therefore, we need to realize that Roosevelt was seriously concerned with economic affairs as well as with power politics, and Taft was aware of America's role as a policeman as well as triumphant businessman. But Wilson has a central importance as one who practically and symbolically integrated all the elements of empire as a way of life. He called for (and began to build) a navy second to none, vigorously supported the expansion of American economic strength, repeatedly intervened (militarily as well as politically) to reform and educate societies that he considered wayward or backward, and boldly undertook to institutionalize the Open Door Policy on a global scale.

Whatever one's judgment of its morality or practicality, and it is open to grave criticism on both counts, it was a grand vision of global benevolence presided over by the United States. To effect that purpose he led the nation into World War I in the righteous conviction that the deployment of American police power was necessary to usher in a millennium of democratic progress based upon the acceptance and observance of the principles and practices of the American marketplace political economy. And Wilson was candid as well as eloquent in explaining his action and his objective.

According to him, the United States entered the conflict in response to violations of its avowed principles "which touched us to the quick and made the life of our own people impossible unless they were corrected *and the world* secured once for all against their recurrence."* Notice well that he did not say that the actions of any power or combination of powers posed a direct, immediate or visceral threat to the security or existence of the United States. His emphasis was *on the world being defined in the image of America*.

"What we demand in this war, therefore, is nothing peculiar to ourselves. It is that the world be made fit and safe to live in; and particularly that it be made safe for every peace-loving nation which, like our own, wishes to live its own life,

*Italics added.

determine its own institutions, be assured of justice and fair dealing. . . . The program of the world's peace, therefore, is our program . . . the only possible program."

Then Wilson echoed Secretary of State Hay with accents borrowed from Presidents Roosevelt and Taft:

"Absolute freedom of navigation upon the seas. . . .

". . . the establishment of an equality of trade conditions among all the nations consenting to the peace. . . .

"A free, open-minded, and absolutely impartial adjustment of all colonial claims, based upon a strict observance of the principle that in determining all such questions of sovereignty the interests of the populations concerned must have equal weight with the equitable claims of the government, whose title is to be determined."

"A general association of nations must be formed under specific covenants for the purpose of affording mutual guarantees of political independence and territorial integrity to great and small states alike."

Wilson not only provided an impressive synthesis of the themes of the new imperial outlook; but, as indicated in his remarks about the old colonial system, he understood the nature of the challenge he had defined. The substance of it was that he had to control the disgruntled poor (symbolized by the ongoing revolutions in China, Mexico, and Russia) while simultaneously policing the greed of the rich who competed with the United States for the wealth of the world. That awesome undertaking was the inevitable result of defining American freedom and welfare and security in global terms.

There were four primary strategies for attaining the objective. The United States could organize and deploy its resources to police the world—or at any rate those parts of it that refused to accept the American conception of benevolent progress. It could treat the poor as equals and support them to control the rich in the short run, confident that American power would prevail in the medium or long run. It could step aside and let the other rich deal with the poor on the assumption that both groups would eventually be forced to accept American leadership. Or it could use its power in alliance with the other rich to control the poor in return for the rich accepting the American rules for the international marketplace.

The last-mentioned option was Wilson's choice, and he sought to confine both confrontations within the Open Door system through the creation of a League of Nations led by the United States. That was his vision of a "new world order," and he tied it to Article X of the League Covenant. "The Members of the League undertake to respect and preserve as against external aggression the territorial integrity and existing political independence of all Members of the League." That, Wilson emphasized, "seems to me to constitute the very backbone of the whole covenant. Without it the League would be hardly more than an influential debating society."

That proposition provoked a traumatic argument among Americans. Wilson ultimately lost because too many people viewed that kind of commitment to the status quo as inevitably involving the United States in an endless recourse to military force or a devolution into old-style empire—or both. The ensuing defeat of the League Treaty (1919–20) forced everyone to reexamine the accepted strategy and tactics—and even the limits—of empire as a way of life.

APPENDIX
American Interventionist Activity
(excluding declared wars) from 1898 to 1920.

1898 Nicaragua—February 7 and 8. To protect American lives and property at San Juan del Sur.

1898–99   China—November 5, 1898, to March 15, 1899. To provide a guard for the legation at Peking and the consulate at Tientsin during contest between the Dowager Empress and her son.

1899   Nicaragua. To protect American interests at San Juan del Norte, February 22 to March 5, and at Bluefields a few weeks later in connection with the insurrection of Gen. Juan P. Reyes.

1899   Samoa—March 13 to May 15. To protect American interests and to take part in a bloody contention over the succession to the throne.

1899–1901   Philippine Islands. To protect American interests following the war with Spain, and to conquer the islands by defeating the Filipinos in their war for independence.

1900   China—May 24 to September 28. To protect foreign lives during the Boxer rising, particularly at Peking. For many years after this experience a permanent legation guard was maintained in Peking, and was strengthened at times as trouble threatened. It was still there in 1934.

1901   Colombia (State of Panama)—November 20 to December 4. To protect American property on the Isthmus and to keep transit lines open during serious revolutionary disturbances.

1902   Colombia—April 16 to 23. To protect American lives and property at Bocas del Toro during a civil war.

1902   Colombia (State of Panama)—September 17 to November 18. To place armed guards on all trains crossing the Isthmus and to keep the railroad line open.

1903   Honduras—March 23 to 30 or 31. To protect the American consulate and the steamship wharf at Puerto Cortez during a period of revolutionary activity.

1903   Dominican Republic—March 30 to April 21. To protect American interests in the city of Santo Domingo during a revolutionary outbreak.

1903   Syria—September 7 to 12. To protect the American consulate in Beirut when a local Moslem uprising was feared.

1903–14   Panama. To protect American interests and lives during and following the revolution for independence from Colombia over construction of the Isthmian canal. With brief intermissions, U.S. Marines were stationed on the Isthmus from November 4, 1903, to January 21, 1914, to guard American interests.

1904   Dominican Republic—January 2 to February 11. To protect American interests in Puerto Plata and Sosua and Santo Domingo City during revolutionary fighting.

1904–5   Korea—January 5, 1904, to November 11, 1905. To guard the American legation in Seoul.

1904   Tangier, Morocco. "We want either Perdicaris alive or Raisuli dead." Demonstration by a squadron to force release of a kidnapped American. Marine guard landed to protect consul general.

1904   Panama—November 17 to 24. To protect American lives and property at Ancon at the time of a threatened insurrection.

1904–05   Korea. Marine guard sent to Seoul for protection during Russo-Japanese war.

1906–09   Cuba—September 1906 to January 23, 1909. Intervention to restore order, protect foreigners, and establish a stable government after serious revolutionary activity.

1907   Honduras—March 18 to June 8. To protect American interests during a war between Honduras and Nicaragua; troops were stationed for a few days or weeks in Trujillo, Ceiba, Puerto Cortez, San Pedro, Laguna, and Choloma.

1910 Nicaragua—February 22. During a civil war, to get information of conditions at Corinto; May 19, to September 4, to protect American interests at Bluefields.

1911 Honduras—January 26 and some weeks thereafter. To protect American lives and interests during a civil war in Honduras.

1911 China. Approaching stages of the nationalist revolution. An ensign and ten men in October tried to enter Wuchang to rescue missionaries but retired on being warned away.

A small landing force guarded American private property and consulate at Hankow in October.

A marine guard was established in November over the cable stations at Shanghai.

Landing forces were sent for protection to Nanking, Chin-kiang, Taku, and elsewhere.

1912 Honduras. Small force landed to prevent seizure by the government of an American-owned railroad at Puerto Cortez. Forces withdrawn after the United States disapproved the action.

1912 Panama. Troops, on request of both political parties, supervised elections outside the Canal Zone.

1912 Cuba—June 5 to August 5. To protect American interests in the Province of Oriente, and Havana.

1912 China—August 24 to 26, on Kentucky Island, and August 26 to 30 at Camp Nicholson. To protect Americans and American interests during revolutionary activity.

1912 Turkey—November 18 to December 3. To guard the American legation at Constantinople during a Balkan war.

1912–25   Nicaragua—August to November 1912. To protect American interests during an attempted revolution. A small force serving as a legation guard and as a promoter of peace and governmental stability, remained until August 5, 1925.

1912–42   China. The disorders which began with the Kuomintang rebellion in 1912, which were redirected by the invasion of China by Japan, and finally ended by war between Japan and the United States in 1941, led to demonstrations and landing parties for protection in China continuously and at many points from 1912 on to 1941. The guard at Peking and along the route to the sea was maintained until 1941. In 1927 the United States had 5,670 troops ashore in China and 44 naval vessels in its waters. In 1933 the U.S. had 3,027 armed men ashore. All this protective action was in general terms based on treaties with China ranging from 1858 to 1901.

1913   Mexico—September 5 to 7. A few marines landed at Claria Estero to aid in evacuating American citizens and others from the Yaqui Valley, made dangerous for foreigners by civil strife.

1914   Haiti—January 29 to February 9, February 20 to 21, October 19. To protect American nationals in a time of dangerous unrest.

1914   Dominican Republic—June and July. During a revolutionary movement, United States naval force by gunfire stopped the bombardment of Puerto Plata, and by threat of force maintained Santo Domingo City as a neutral zone.

1914–17   Mexico. The undeclared Mexican-American hostilities following the Dolphin affair and Villa's raids included capture of Vera Cruz and later Pershing's expedition into northern Mexico.

1915–34   Haiti—July 28, 1915, to August 15, 1934. To maintain order during a period of chronic and threatened insurrection.

1916–24   Dominican Republic—May 1916 to September 1924. To maintain order during a period of chronic and threatened insurrection.

1917–33   Cuba. To protect American interests during an insurrection and subsequent unsettled conditions. Most of the United States armed force left Cuba by August 1919, but two companies remained at Camaguey until February 1922.

1918–19   Mexico. After withdrawal of the Pershing expedition, our troops entered Mexico in pursuit of bandits at least three times in 1918 and six times in 1919. In August 1918 American and Mexican troops fought at Nogales.

1918–20   Soviet Russia. Marines were landed at and near Vladivostok in June and July to protect the American consulate and other points in the fighting between the Bolsheviki troops and the Czech army which had traversed Siberia from the western front. A joint proclamation of emergency government and neutrality was issued by the American, Japanese, British, French, and Czech commanders in July and the American party remained until late August.

   In August the project expanded. Then 7,000 men were landed in Vladivostok and remained until January 1920, as part of an allied occupational force.

   In September 1918, 5,000 American troops joined the allied intervention force at Archangel, suffered 500 casualties, and remained until June 1919.

   A handful of marines took part earlier in a British landing on the Murmansk coast (near Norway) but only incidentally.

All these operations were to offset effects of the Bolsheviki revolution in Russia and were partly supported by Tzarist or Kerensky elements. No war was declared.

1919 Honduras—September 3 to 12. A landing force was sent ashore to maintain order in a neutral zone during an attempted revolution.

CHAPTER SEVEN
A Long Debate About the Nature and Limits of Empire

The prosperity of the United States depends upon the economic settlements which may be made in Europe and the key to the future is with those who make and control those settlements.

SECRETARY OF STATE CHARLES EVANS HUGHES, 1921

It sometimes amuses me when people say, "settle the Mexican question." You and I know that neither the Mexican nor the Cuban question will be "settled" in the lifetime of any one now living.

DWIGHT MORROW to GENERAL ENOCH H. CROWDER, 1929

It would be particularly unwise from political and psychological standpoints to permit limitation of our action to be imposed by any other nation than our own.

PRESIDENT FRANKLIN DELANO ROOSEVELT, 1933

Our trade agreements program will automatically put economic pressure on Germany, and in this we have a ready forged weapon in hand to induce Germany to meet world trade and political sentiment.

State Department Memorandum, 1938

As FAR AS foreign affairs were concerned, most Americans interpreted President Warren G. Harding's promise to return to "normalcy" as a commitment to follow a less crusading foreign policy. They were not only weary of Wilson's big war to force the future, as contrasted with McKinley's splendid little war against Spain (which in their view had merely ratified the inevitable), but they wanted to enjoy the benefits of the existing empire while watching it fulfill its natural destiny in its own time. Secretary of State Charles Evans Hughes caught the spirit perfectly: "We simply wish peace and order and stability and recognition of honest rights properly acquired so that this hemisphere may not only be the hemisphere of peace but the hemisphere of international justice."

Hughes was not signaling a fundamental shift from an imperial to a non- or anti-imperial way of life. He was merely expressing deep skepticism about the Wilsonian conception of how to deal with change, and the general desire to relax while building a less dramatic but more enduring "community of interest" among the rich nations that would sustain empire as a way of life. Thus he and like-minded leaders were willing to reduce armaments, back away from Wilson's military interventions, and trust in the imperial power of the American political economy. Given the nature of American strength, it was a sane and sophisticated strategy.

Precisely for that reason, however, it evoked various kinds of opposition at home and abroad. The poor nations saw themselves condemned either to continued poverty or a modest prosperity paid for with the destruction of their own cultures. The rich countries feared sliding into middle-class dependence—welfare without power—upon the United States. Various domestic groups wanted a more activist policy. And those few who sought to end the imperial way of life viewed the Hughes approach as the most insidious danger of all. The competitive interplay among those groups made it impossible for men like Hughes and Herbert C. Hoover to put their strategy into operation as effectively as they developed it as a theory and policy.

Such difficulties led many later observers to conclude that those men were naïve, misguided, or simply mistaken; and on those grounds to dismiss them as irrelevant, even to charge them with responsibility for America's subsequent troubles. The reality was significantly different. Another massive breakdown of marketplace capitalism in 1929–30 generated among the rich as well as the poor countries strong opposition to that classic system.

In that situation, American leaders had one basic option. They could take the lead in devising a new political economy, or they could oppose those nations (especially Germany and Japan) which sought to change the existing system. After considerable debate, leaders like Franklin Delano Roosevelt and Cordell Hull chose the latter course of action and thereby propelled empire as a way of life on to its grandiose climax.

I

Though not as evangelical in tone, the debate about American foreign policy during the 1920s and 1930s was in many ways more informative and revealing than the confrontation over the Versailles Peace Treaty. For one thing, it clarified the crucial differences of opinion that defeated Wilson's grand plan for "a new world order." It also made it clear that most Americans still expected their country to inform and guide the development of the world, even if they had decided to become plainclothesmen rather than cops on the corner.

The urges to empire that had been so dramatically personified by Roosevelt and Wilson did not disappear. It was rather like the end of a laboratory experiment that begins with putting fine iron filings and chalk in a beaker filled with a liquid. Shaken vigorously, they fly about in a mad swirl that looks like a gray storm cloud. Stop the agitation, and they settle out each to its own. The iron filings still wanted militant imperial action, and the chalk still wanted to reform the world. But now they were arguing with each other rather than creating a cloud of progressive imperialism.

Both groups were visible on the scene—particularly in discussions about how to deal with the poor nations which demanded a more equitable and consequential share of the world's wealth—but the fundamental issues and terms of debate were determined by other American leaders. The dialogue about how to cope with those present or future revolutionaries was not at all incidental, but it can best be understood in the context of the broad argument about how to sustain the natural growth of the empire.

One powerful group of people, symbolized by the House of Morgan, took the *very* long view. They believed in the power of finance. They also had traditional ties with European bankers. Trusting in such strength and connections, particularly in London, they were willing in the short run to work through their friendly neighborhood bankers on the assumption that they would ultimately take over the business. They therefore concentrated their unilateral activities in the western hemisphere, and hence never made a serious, sustained effort to establish a truly competitive world banking system.

Many manufacturers disagreed. Their experience between 1893 and 1914 prompted them to distrust big bankers. The war boom had enabled them to repay most or all of their debts to the financiers, and they relished their independence. Thus they wanted the government to help them secure and expand that liberty. They pressured Washington, for example, to insist that any money loaned to foreigners should be spent in their American factories. They were particularly upset because the British were known to insist upon such "tied" loans, and they felt that bankers were being hypocritical: it was all right for London but not for America. And the most militant imperial manufacturers wanted Washington to collect the wartime debts to America by having various kinds of property—in the colonies as well as in the European mother countries—transferred to their corporate control and profit.

Other vigorous advocates of empire emphasized the importance of managing—or overthrowing—the revolutions in China, Mexico, and Russia. Most of those individuals and corporations, like William F. Buckley and Judge F. J. Kearful, and Standard Oil, evolved their policies within a very narrow framework. They wanted to keep the land, oil, and other wealth that they had acquired and do with it as they pleased. And in the process teach the natives a lesson that would intimidate other poor nations.

However restricted that attitude may appear, it was nevertheless part of a strong tradition that was rooted deeply in the 19th century, and it had been supported by many people who understood the broader ramifications of non-capitalist conceptions of property. Professor Weinberg discussed their outlook in terms of the destined or proper use of the soil, for example, noting that Captain Mahan became increasingly concerned about the threat to the capitalist *system* posed by revolutionary nationalism.

Those people saw specific issues of property—say a railroad or a loan in China, a factory in Russia, or oil wells or silver mines or farm land in Mexico—as part of a global system of capitalism. The system—even specific entrepreneurs—could tolerate the loss of this, that, or the other investment or loan, but it could not survive countries taking themselves out of the system. Such action did not have to be socialist or communist in motive, rhetoric, or aim to threaten the empire. As with the Mexicans, who grounded their action in ancient ideals of community, any contracting out of the global marketplace threatened both the theory and the practice of capitalism.

The most militant imperialists emphasized the necessity for prompt and strong action to prevent such withdrawals from the global system. But the more sophisticated leaders, whatever their moral attitude toward such intervention, realized that the pragmatic consequences of the hard-line strategy involved war and more war. Such conflict not only disrupted the functioning of the capitalist system per se; but, as they concluded from their analysis of World War I, war was a hothouse for revolutionary change. Hence their objective was to establish, consolidate, and develop a limited, responsible, honorable and reasonably equitable empire which could in time evolve a working relationship with revolutionary societies like Mexico, China, and even Russia. Some of the most perceptive of those leaders, such as Hoover, had a sense of History: a realization that revolutionary enthusiasms did cool down, and that the revolutionaries became ever more concerned with conserving what they had created.

That approach, or strategy, involved an extremely difficult

process. The effort, whether undertaken by Americans or any other imperial peoples, depends upon establishing two essential conditions. *The first is for the imperial culture to admit that it is an empire.* That clears the mind and psyche of rationalizations about expansion extending the area of freedom and liberty; minimizes the distortions of perception and thought produced by self-righteousness; and enables people to discuss the national interest in concrete, specific terms rather than as if everything that happens in the world poses a threat to the national security.

The second prerequisite is to minimize (and, if possible, abandon) the imperial propensity to externalize evil. One of the major characteristics of an imperial way of life is its tendency to define domestic problems and difficulties, and to explain the failure to resolve them, in terms of external developments. Empire turns a culture away from its own life as a society or community. Ultimately, everything is seen primarily in terms of foreigners; the culture considers itself embattled and beleaguered, and hence unable to define or deal with reality in ways that are appropriate and effective.

No policy-making leaders of the 1920s and 1930s ever made those points in precisely that way (though a few of them like Hoover and Dwight W. Morrow occasionally spoke in very similar terms), but they did understand what was required to prevent the imperial way of life from becoming a self-destructive monomania. That was, after all, the fundamental reason why Hoover, Hughes, and others opposed Wilson's conception of America as the end-all and be-all of the future. Hughes provided an excellent example of their outlook. The Treaty, and especially Article X, "makes no allowance for changes which may be desirable. It ascribes a prescience and soundness of judgment . . . which nobody in the history of the world has ever possessed." It "attempts to make permanent existing conditions . . . in a world of dynamic forces to which no one can set bounds." Wilson was profoundly and dangerously mistaken in proposing "the attempted compulsion of an inflexible rule." Change was inevitable, and it would be dealt with more safely and effectively by creating an American-led community of "ideals, interests, and purposes."

Three developments intensified the efforts of Hughes, Hoover, and their compatriots to build such a community: the renewed drive by the British, French, and Japanese to strengthen and extend their empires in the eastern Mediterranean and Asia; the problem of rehabilitation in Europe (which was compounded by another postwar breakdown of marketplace capitalism in America during 1920–21); and the need to deal with revolutionary nationalism. "The prosperity of the United States," Hughes explained, "depends upon the economic settlements which may be made in Europe and the key to the future is with those who make and control those settlements." He was determined to obtain "effective recognition of the open door policy of equal commercial opportunity."

Hoover, who was particularly concerned about the devastating decline in American agriculture after the war (prices of the leading crops dropped by about 67 percent) and the high rate of unemployment (10 to 12 percent) took the lead in devising and coordinating a wide range of policies to deal with the crisis. As Secretary of Commerce he began a long campaign to control foreign loans by private bankers, toyed with the idea of a government reconstruction loan to Europe, sought to regularize the overseas investment of profits, launched a battle against "fraud, waste and loss," and floated a suggestion for a public works program. He was too imaginative, too far out ahead. So in the end he settled for disarmament. To his mind not only would it decrease the chances for another war in the short run, but it would free European capital for productive investment and the purchase of various American surpluses.

The Secretary of Commerce did not initiate the campaign for disarmament. On balance it seems likely that the women's movement provided the primary push. And, within that framework, the dynamic force was provided by Dorothy Detzer and others who organized the Women's League for Peace and Freedom. Given that mix of emotions, ideals, and interests, it seems wise to clarify the term *disarmament*.

In its strict, irreducible meaning, disarmament involves limiting The State's monopoly of force to only those weapons required to maintain domestic order. But, given the traditional acceptance of the right of self-defense, disarmament is defined by the ability to repulse an attack on the homeland. In Hoover's mind, the purpose of armanents was to ensure "that no foreign soldier will land on American soil." To "maintain greater forces is not only economic injury to our people but a threat against our neighbors and would be a righteous cause for ill will amongst them."

Other leaders (I have earlier called them soft imperialists) agreed with that proposition. Russell C. Leffingwell, a Wall Street attorney who shared his thoughts with other giants like S. Parker Gilbert and Thomas W. Lamont, put it this way. "We should not only set an example by disarming ourselves, but we should insist on seeing that example followed by refusing credits to those countries which persist in undermining their financial strength by wasteful expenditures on arms and armies." And the Federal Reserve *Bulletin* of December 1921 provided an authoritative footnote: reduce spending for arms to generate economic recovery, stability, and growth.

That analysis and dialogue produced the Washington Conference on disarmament and related matters. With great presence, Hughes pre-empted the discussion with a unilateral commitment to reduce American naval power. The Secretary knew exactly what he was about, and the treaties that emerged from those discussions gave the United States two victories. First, the United States Navy was granted formal equality with the Royal Navy (and superiority over the Japanese), and the government proceeded to exploit that opportunity to develop the most sophisticated fleet afloat. The astute admirals scrapped many rusty and obsolete hulks; built two new battleships and two new carriers; shifted from coal to oil; leapfrogged into new electric power systems; began building a new submarine fleet; and integrated air power into sea power with magnificent ships (and aircrews) like the *Lexington* and the *Saratoga*. Philip T. Rosen is correct: "after all the hoopla subsided, the nation possessed an impressive and modern fleet."

Second, the quiet deployment of American imperial power at the conference led on to other victories. Hughes called on the delegates to respect and meet "the challenge of imperative economic demands." He meant that it was time to bow gracefully to the imperatives of the American empire. And so they did: the British and French agreed to open the door to the oil in the Middle Eastern areas they had monopolized (a triumph that symbolized the acceptance of the Open Door Policy for all raw materials); Japan bowed to American stipulations for loans in the Far East; and the United States was deferred to in Latin America. In return, the bankers in New York and officials in Washington funded European capitalism through the loans and other arrangements incident to the Dawes Plan (1924) and the Young Plan (1929).

American leaders had more difficulty in devising a workable accommodation with revolutionary movements. Most historians, myself included, have generally approached that aspect of imperial policy by focusing on the American response to the Bolshevik Revolution. That is not wrong; for between the years 1917 and 1920, and again after 1941, the Soviet Union did define the issue in the minds and emotions of the key policy-makers in the United States. And, for that matter, what Hoover called "the specter of Bolshevism" haunted their dealings with all other challenges to the global capitalist marketplace.

But during the interwar years the Soviets were largely viewed as a symbolic or potential problem. It was an annoying goad to other troublemakers around the world, but the Bolsheviks were desperately weak and primarily concerned with problems at home. Lenin and his successors caused significant trouble only through their influence in China, where their example, ideas, counsel, and aid did influence one wing of the revolutionary movement. But that challenge was dealt with—at least for the moment—according to the strategy and tactics evolved in coping with Mexico: support the conservative nationalists against the radical nationalists.

It was an obvious strategy, once the Wilsonian nightmare of a new world order had faded from the mind, and a good many people helped to translate the idea into policy. On balance, however, Hoover was the informing presence. He did not conduct the formal negotiations, let alone write the daily dispatches, but his attitude and analysis guided the process. Let us begin with his overview: "a large part of the world had come to believe that they were in the presence of the birth of a new imperial power [the United States] intent upon dominating the destinies and freedom of other people." Hoover was unequivocally and publicly opposed to that idea of a global American empire: it is "not a part of my conception of international relations." He "absolutely disapproved" of the United States presuming to be Big Brother to the western hemisphere or the world.

A good many American imperialists have said that at one time or another. Hoover went beyond the words. He understood that imperial expansion without standards, without honor, without rationality, without responsibility, and without a serious effort to create equity would guarantee the end of the empire. If loans and other investments were not productive for the entire society, then they would become causes of revolutionary nationalism. They would create imbalances in the political economy of the poor countries and generate emotional, cultural, and political ferment. The resulting unrest would bring forth demands within the imperial metropolis for intervention and so lead on to war and more war.

Hoover was putting his own remarkable imprint on what Elihu Root had pointed out back in 1905: the issue was whether or not, "the door, being open, shall lead to something." Root wrote that classically imperial phrase—truly a gem the equal of anything by Winston Churchill—as instructions to American agents at the Algeçiras Conference. Go for the jugular. The fundamental issue was to change Moroccan society so that the United States (and other rich countries) could transform that culture into a dependent part of the world capitalist marketplace:

"Intercourse with that country demands the existence of internal conditions favorable thereto. Security of life and property; equality of opportunities for trade with all natives . . . improvement of the condition of the people that will enable them to profit by the opportunities of foreign traffic . . . and the power to repress subversive disorder and preserve the public peace. . . . People shall be made in a measure fit and able to profit by the advantages [of being integrated into the imperial system]."

The American imperial way of life was thereby revealed, once and for all, as not simply a matter of equal opportunity with other imperial powers to engage in innocent trade. *It inherently involved, knowingly and purposively, the destruction of traditional values and their replacement with arbitrarily imposed external values.* No surprise that the natives resisted.

Hoover understood all that: he had been party to the American capitalist empire in Australia, Russia, and China. He had learned that Wilson was wrong about trying to "teach" them: it was better to go into the classroom and learn along with them. Hence Hoover concentrated on what Root called improving "the condition of the people." That was his definition of a productive loan or a productive investment. He was extremely critical of bankers and other people who did not honor that principle. And very reluctant to intervene to protect their money or property.

Granted, this man Hoover seems strange. We are not accustomed to being told that enough is enough; particularly in our context of Korea, Cuba, and Vietnam. But Hoover was not an isolated eccentric. Listen to the financier Thomas Lamont. "The theory of collecting debts by gunboat is unrighteous, unworkable, and obsolete." And so, despite much opposition and skepticism, Dwight Morrow (a friend and colleague of Lamont) was sent along to Mexico to negotiate an accommodation with the revolutionary world.

Here was a group of American leaders who recognized the limits of empire. They were not pacifists. They were not even anti-imperialists in any meaningful sense. We might even agree (though it is debatable) that they would have gone on in the spirit of Roosevelt and Wilson if China, Mexico, and Russia had not broken a few spokes in the wheels of empire. And without any doubt they were elitist, prejudiced, and determined to save all they could of empire as a way of life.

But they had no Rooseveltian or Wilsonian illusions about the United States reforming, setting right, or policing the entire world. Morrow sought only to come to the best possible terms with the new Mexican world aborning. He and Hoover, and their compatriots, were in truth remarkable people. They recognized that they were riding the wave across one age into another. None of them particularly liked the truth they knew. But they faced it squarely.

When the Japanese invaded Manchuria in 1931, Hoover said the future of China was the responsibility of the Chinese. Morrow had a lighter touch. "It sometimes amuses me," he had earlier commented privately to the American proconsul in Cuba, "when people say, 'settle the Mexican question.' You and I know that neither the Mexican nor the Cuban question will be 'settled' in the lifetime of any one now living."

II

Morrow died soon after speaking that wisdom. Hence no one will ever know how he would have responded to the subsequent 1929 crisis of the American political economy. The imperial capitalist system again flunked the course. It is silly to take seriously the charge that leaders like Hoover were to blame. The heart of it is that the faith in growth was once again dashed to the ground.

The failure stunned most Americans. They had been born to the truth that their culture was predicated upon growth, and now there was no growth. Truly a traumatic experience. Statistics can help to reveal the consequences of that failure, but it was essentially a collage of desperate human experiences. Some people died of starvation. Many died of malnutrition. And millions barely survived, their bodies and spirits stunted for life.

The psychological impact of the Great Depression deeply affected American foreign policy, particularly because Franklin Delano Roosevelt's New Deal did not generate peacetime recovery—let alone a new burst of growth and prosperity. Most Americans realized, privately if not publicly, that the economy was revived only through World War II. As a consequence, they were viscerally uneasy about a slide back into depression after the conflict ended.

That nagging doubt and uncertainty was reinforced by the knowledge that the depression had forced even the United States to begin limiting the marketplace freedoms that were considered the foundation of individual liberty. Despite their periodic support for social and other reforms, Americans had little psychological affinity for institutional limits on their freedom of action; *or for a philosophy that viewed such restraints as part of a community of reciprocal benefits and obligations*. Such restrictions were tolerable only under conditions of economic growth that rendered them incidental. And in the American political economy that growth was predicated upon imperial expansion.

Those attitudes prompted most Americans to view the efforts by other countries, Great Britain and France as well as Germany and Japan, to deal with the depression through various controls and plans as threatening to leave the United States a beleaguered island of freedom. That led to a convoluted pattern of thinking between 1929 and 1949. The planning of the depression years was viewed as an example of the dangerous influence of the revolution in Russia, and later, of Nazi Germany; and so, after Hitler was defeated, the Soviet Union was pictured as another Nazi Germany.

The New Deal's relatively disjointed efforts to deal with the depression were not successful in ending the crisis, but they affected the conduct of foreign relations in four important ways. First, and from the outset, Roosevelt steadily increased military spending as part of the effort to revive the system. He initially concentrated on the navy (his first move in 1933 was to build 32 ships over three years), but later extended his largesse to the army and the air force. The emphasis was striking: between 1932 and 1940 roughly 20 percent of government tax *receipts* were fed to the military.

As part of that, and regardless of one's judgment about the necessity or the wisdom of it, Roosevelt reinforced the inherent power of the giant corporations. By the end of the decade, for example, companies in four states received 39.32

percent of all military contracts; and fifteen states accounted for 82.85 percent of the total. That was not at all unrelated to the revelation in 1939 that 52 percent of total assets were owned by just 0.1 percent of all corporations. In the broader, structural sense the New Deal created an institutional link, between the huge companies and the military.

Second, and whatever the reforms and regulations that emerged, let alone Roosevelt's campaign rhetoric about "malefactors of great wealth," his administration was concerned to save and if possible revitalize a capitalist political economy based on the large corporations. Neither the President nor any of his consequential associates had any interest in moving the system toward some kind of socialism or backward into laissez-faire. As a result, foreign policy was dealt with in the traditional framework.

Which meant, third, that power became ever more consolidated and centralized. All the talk, both then and later, about whether or not Roosevelt wanted to be a dictator in the democratic idiom was largely beside the point. He finigled and fanagled and in the end did pretty much what he wanted to do: losing far fewer than he won. Think only of his successful manipulation of the budget to obtain ever higher military expenditures. But that does not make him a dictator. He was simply a charming upper-class disingenuous leader who understood that marketplace capitalism had proved incapable of functioning without being subsidized by the taxpayer. And he could not imagine anything beyond saving marketplace capitalism.

His tax programs, for example, soaked the middle- and lower-class citizens with a ruthlessness not exhibited by any conservative President in the history of the republic. The truth of it was (and remains) that Adam Smith had been proved wrong. There was no Hidden Hand magically setting it all right. The State and the large corporations had become, in the marvelous phrase coined by historian Alfred D. Chandler, Jr., the Very Visible Hands financed by the ordinary citizens.

Lacking the elementary candor to admit that marketplace capitalism had failed, American leaders had no recourse but to employ The State to create markets, control raw materials, and accumulate capital. And also to provide essential social services (from education to social work and on to death benefits), including sustaining the unemployed at the lowest effective level. And so the taxpayer came to pay twice. Once by providing the profits to the corporations and then again through his taxes which also helped the corporations avoid paying their full share of the welfare costs.

That effort to save the system was unquestionably humane. And certainly necessary. After all, an empire in the name of freedom cannot allow people to die in the streets. But the New Deal also changed the nature of politics—and hence the substance of policy-making. The essence of politics, *the process of defining and choosing between alternatives*, became increasingly restricted to and centralized within the federal government and the giant corporations. Alternatives were anti-American because they were anti-imperial.

The groups that I defined earlier as constituting The State were being transformed. Some were losing power and effectiveness, and others were being buried within the executive department and its administrative bureaucracy. And the members of the Congress, and local and state governments, let alone the citizens themselves, were being steadily reduced to responding to, or simply implementing, proposals and actions taken by the executive department and the corporations.

Thus the collapse of the system of marketplace capitalism consolidated the power of those who were committed to sustaining the system. That is not to discount the marginal rewards of the reforms. The point is that, while it was a New Deal, it was *not* a different game. The imperial outlook had once again become a vision of progress for everyone.

III

Franklin Roosevelt understood the ultimate truth about empire as a way of life. End the empire and all hell might break loose: the Furies would appear. Thus neither he nor his close advisers could abide people who suggested that it was time—either morally or pragmatically—to consider and devise an alternative to that way of life. As a Wilsonian, Roosevelt clearly perceived America as a benevolent and progressive policeman, and saw no contradiction between that role and being a good neighbor.

The President preferred to secure America's objectives with a smile, a wink, a fatherly talk, a shrewd compromise, or a nudge. And, if those proved insufficient, he liked to deploy imperial power indirectly: say through the threat of military and economic intervention exercised—to use an appropriate naval idiom—hull down over the horizon. To that extent, he had matured beyond the imperial enthusiasms he displayed while serving under Wilson. "Sooner or later," he observed in those days, "it seems the United States must go down there and clean up the Mexican political mess."

Thus he dealt with the revolutionary turmoil in Cuba during 1933–34 by surrounding the island with American ships, refusing to recognize the moderately leftist government that came to power, and then signing favorable political and economic agreements with its far more conservative successor. Similar strategies were later employed against Mexico and other Latin American countries. And at least tried in dealings with various major nations.

One of Roosevelt's closer advisers described the substance of that police power with admirable candor. "No government" in the western hemisphere, remarked Sumner Welles, "can survive for a protracted period without recognition of the United States." One can hardly imagine a more deft description of empire without using the word *empire*. Every foreign government, and many of their citizens, understood American policy in that light. Depending upon their mood, they considered it quixotic or hypocritical to exercise such power over others while denying that it was imperial.

The Japanese took it more seriously because the United States refused to recognize their sphere of interest in Manchuria, and had further used its economic power to block various Japanese projects in China. Beyond that, the Japanese economy depended in a consequential way on American raw materials that made it vulnerable to such pressure. But Roosevelt, Secretary of State Cordell Hull, and other officials denied that Latin America was a sphere of interest, and refused even to discuss the legitimacy of a Japanese Monroe Doctrine. They instead reiterated the American commitment to the Open Door Policy and continued to demand that Japan pull back from China as a *precondition* for substantive negotiations about economic and other matters.

Prejudice—even racism—informed the American attitude. More accurately, those elements honed the basic economic opposition to a particularly deadly edge. After all, the United States had several times fought "white" Europeans over the same issues. In any event, the American posture— later called negotiating from strength—amounted to saying give us what is most important to us and then we will talk about what is left. Understandably, that approach did not appeal to the Japanese. They felt that they were being asked to surrender one solution to their economic problems without a commitment from the United States to provide an effective alternative. That reading of the situation was reinforced, moreover, by Washington's response to the efforts of other countries to deal with the crisis of the depression.

The United States had responded unfavorably, for example, to Great Britain's move in 1932 to create a trading bloc known as the Imperial Preference System composed of its colonies and other members of that global sphere of interest known as the Commonwealth. Secretary of State Hull immediately launched a counterattack; and, when Britain's need for massive aid became imperative in 1941, effectively deployed America's economic power to force London to accept the Open Door Policy.

The Roosevelt administration had reacted in the same way when, in 1934, Germany instituted strict controls on foreign trade. Germany made repeated efforts during the next five years to negotiate a series of bilateral economic agreements, but Hull refused even to discuss the matter unless there was "a fundamental acceptance by Germany of our trade philosophy." One of the Secretary's associates described the result as "closely approaching trade warfare." As the London *Times* commented, "continuous friction was inevitable."

Each of those encounters grew out of America's commitment to unfettered access to the markets and resources of the world, and its growing sense of urgency about gaining those objectives. For a time, even as late as 1938, the State Department felt that the campaign to build a system on that basis would prove successful against Germany as well as Japan. "Our trade agreements program will automatically put economic pressure on Germany, and in this we have a ready forged weapon in hand to induce Germany to meet world trade and political sentiment." One hardly needs to emphasize the key point: American leaders had equated their imperial policy with world sentiment.

As Roosevelt acknowledged, however, such economic pressure moved too slowly. And, as Japan and Germany extended their use of military power, American leaders increasingly emphasized their earlier fears that a world divided into such trading blocs would create what Walter Lippmann called "a truly revolutionary condition" that would force the United States to make structural and institutional changes at home. "Unless a system of open trade becomes firmly established," warned Hull, "there will be chronic political instability and recurrent economic collapse." Small wonder that John D. Rockefeller, Jr., worked overtime to create an Interchurch World Movement to provide insurance for overseas investments, and in general underwrite "the prosperity of the country and the future stability of our government."

Not all Americans agreed with the Roosevelt administration's doomsday interpretation of the situation. Those critics vigorously expressed their opposition to what they viewed as a strong drift—or march—into war. Although they were often lumped together as isolationists by the Roosevelt administration and its supporters, they actually offered a wide variety of proposals which often conflicted with each other. The only thing that united them was their opposition to military intervention in the European war prior to the Japanese attack on Pearl Harbor.

A minuscule minority was composed of practicing pacifists who honored their faith after America went to war. A somewhat larger number were often mistaken for pacifists but only opposed war up to the point the United States was attacked. Others took the same position but drew their line around the entire western hemisphere. Still another segment of the opposition concentrated as much on attacking what they considered to be the insidious and invidious influence on foreign policy enjoyed by bankers and corporations, or the disingenuousness of Roosevelt, as on developing any concrete or coherent policy alternative.

A wide range of such plans were supported by shifting coalitions among the anti-interventionists. Some were almost classical 19th-century imperialists, proposing to sit tight behind the navy (or under an umbrella of airpower) until the Europeans and the Asians exhausted themselves. Then

America could establish its global system and usher in a new imperial millennium. Others concluded that any effort to enforce the Open Door Policy on a global scale would inevitably produce war after war after war. They proposed to settle for primacy within regional spheres of influence and negotiate economic and political agreements with other such blocs. That approach hardly qualified as an anti-expansionist outlook, but it did represent a willingness to settle for less than global supremacy. Finally, a significant number of so-called isolationists were ready (even eager) to have a showdown with Japan but wanted to stay out of the European conflict.

Those who supported Roosevelt's various actions—many of them arbitrary and some of them dishonest—that steadily increased the probability of war came to defend the President on the grounds that it was impossible to have a useful debate with such a hodge-podge of mutually contradictory critics. Given that situation, he had no choice but to do whatever he considered necessary, through any means that were effective, to ensure the security of the country.

One can sympathize with that attitude, but it does not change the essential facts of the situation. Roosevelt and his supporters had a basic responsibility to open a candid discussion of the nature and consequences of empire as a way of life. The issues were not so inherently complex or obscure as to make it impossible to articulate them clearly, and the effort would in and of itself have forced the critics to address the fundamentals.

The President did not do so. And between the January 1940 termination of the commercial treaty with Japan and the September 1940 exchange of destroyers for bases with Great Britain, he committed the government to a war for America's imperial way of life. He shipped War Department arms to Britain, established a Defense Research Committee, brought leading Republican interventionists into the cabinet, approved a bill calling for a 70 percent increase in the navy, and was preparing to outline American war aims. His new Secretary of War, Henry L. Stimson, said it all: the United States government had placed itself at the head of a "sherriff's posse."

By then there was nothing left to debate. The issue had been reduced to a matter of how and when the fighting would begin. That happened first in the Atlantic as Roosevelt deployed the navy against German submarines. But the decision had been made to go to war in Asia if Japan moved to control the resources of Southeast Asia. The Japanese resolved that matter by moving simultaneously against France and Britain in that region to obtain the oil and rubber, and against the American fleet at Pearl Harbor.

APPENDIX
American Interventionist Activity
(excluding declared wars) from 1920 to 1941.

1920–22   Russia (Siberia)—February 16, 1920 to November 19, 1922. A marine guard to protect the United States radio station and property on Russian Island, Bay of Vladivostok.

1920   China—March 14. A landing force was sent ashore for a few hours to protect lives during a disturbance at Kiukiang.

1920   Guatemala—April 9 to 27. To protect the American legation and other American interests, such as the cable station, during a period of fighting between Unionists and the government of Guatemala.

1921   Panama-Costa Rica. American naval squadrons demonstrated in April on both sides of the Isthmus to prevent war between the two countries over a boundary dispute.

1922 Turkey—September and October. A landing force was sent ashore with consent of both Greek and Turkish authorities to protect American lives and property when the Turkish nationalists entered Smyrna.

1924 Honduras—February 28 to March 31, September 10 to 15. To protect American lives and interests during election hostilities.

1924 China—September. Marines were landed to protect Americans and other foreigners in Shanghai during Chinese factional hostilities.

1925 China—January 15 to August 29. Fighting of Chinese factions accompanied by riots and demonstrations in Shanghai necessitated landing American forces to protect lives and property in the International Settlement.

1925 Honduras—April 19 to 21. To protect foreigners at La Ceiba during a political upheaval.

1925 Panama—October 12 to 23. Strikes and rent riots led to the landing of about 600 American troops to keep order and protect American interests.

1926–33 Nicaragua—May 7 to June 5, 1926; August 27, 1926 to January 3, 1933. The coup d'état of General Chamorro aroused revolutionary activities leading to the landing of American marines to protect the interests of the United States. United States forces came and went, but seem not to have left the country entirely until January 3, 1933. Their work included activity against the outlaw leader Sandino in 1926.

1926 China—August and September. The Nationalist attack on Hankow necessitated the landing of American naval forces to protect American citizens. A small guard was maintained at the consulate general's even after September 16, when the rest of the forces were withdrawn. Likewise, when Nationalist forces captured Kiukiang, naval forces were landed for the protection of foreigners November 4 to 6.

1927   China—February. Fighting at Shanghai caused American naval forces and marines to be increased there. In March a naval guard was stationed at the American consulate at Nanking after Nationalist forces captured the city. American and British destroyers later used shell fire to protect Americans and other foreigners. "Following this incident additional forces of marines and naval vessels were ordered to China and stationed in the vicinity of Shanghai and Tientsin."

1933   Cuba. During a revolution against President Gerardo Machado naval forces demonstrated but no landing was made.

1940   Newfoundland, Bermuda, St. Lucia, Bahamas, Jamaica, Antigua, Trinidad, and British Guiana. Troops were sent to guard air and naval bases obtained by negotiation with Great Britain. These were sometimes called lend-lease bases.

1941   Greenland. Taken under protection of the United States in April.

1941   Netherlands (Dutch Guiana). In November the President ordered American troops to occupy Dutch Guiana but by agreement with the Netherlands government in exile. Brazil cooperated to protect aluminum ore supply from the bauxite mines in Surinam.

1941   Iceland. Taken under the protection of the United States, with consent of its government, for strategic reasons.

1941   Germany. Sometime in the spring the President ordered the navy to patrol ship lanes to Europe. By July our warships were convoying and by September were attacking German submarines. There was no authorization of Congress or declaration of war.

CHAPTER EIGHT

Once Again the Benevolent, Progressive Policeman

Somebody . . . made an awful mistake in bringing about a situation where Russia was permitted to come out of a war with the power she will have.

SECRETARY OF STATE JAMES BYRNES, 1945

The theme of American participation in World War II was victory at the lowest possible cost.

HISTORIAN STEPHEN E. AMBROSE, 1971

We can't do business with Stalin.

PRESIDENT FRANKLIN D. ROOSEVELT, March 23, 1945

Our fingers will be in every pie.

SENATOR ROBERT A. TAFT, 1943

ALL THAT followed flowed from Roosevelt's decision about how to define and fight the war, and from the reality and related psychological scars of the Great Depression. The President was determined to destroy German and Japanese power. His policy reaffirmed the commitment, born of the Civil War, to a strategy of annihilation unto unconditional surrender. He likewise proposed to wage that war as cheaply as possible and with the least possible disruption of domestic life and society. And he undertook to attain those objectives in the name of preserving and extending America's traditional values, thus realizing its global dream of an open world marketplace dominated by American power.

It was a grand illusion predicated upon a failure to comprehend the full meaning of the Great Depression, and grounded in the charming belief that the United States could reap the rewards of empire without paying the costs of empire and without admitting that it was an empire. As a result, the benevolent, progressive policeman became ever less benevolent and progressive—and ever more baffled and frustrated when other nations increasingly challenged his legitimacy and authority.

I

There was never any question about the President's desire, as historian John Morton Blum has described it, to win "the war as fast and as thoroughly as possible." And to do so, as Stephen Ambrose comments, "at the lowest possible cost." Nor was there anything morally or pragmatically questionable about that approach. No rational and responsible leader wants to waste lives or dally along the bloody trail to victory. The real issue involves the cost to be paid for cutting it too fine. Not in the sense of *losing*, but in winning while entertaining illusions of grandeur or omnipotence and at the same time increasing the odds against realizing those fantasies.

In and of themselves, "thoroughly," "fast," and "lowest possible" cost are almost logically incompatible. Roosevelt assured that judgment by attempting simultaneously to avoid all possible disruption of the fabric of existing American culture. It was not so much a policy of guns and butter as it was a dream of more of the same. Combining the least rocking of the boat with the other objectives created an inherently irreconcilable combination of methods and goals.

Winning completely, for example, meant honoring the strategy and tactics of unconditional surrender that Lincoln and Grant had distilled from much blood. It required concentrating vast force on the vitals of the enemy at the price of heavy losses. Many people thought that the deployment of overwhelming air power would achieve the objective at a relatively low body count. And planes and bombs did contribute to complete victory. But not quite in the way the prophets promised. *Air power proved effective only as it enabled the infantry to kill enemy soldiers and occupy their territory.*

Dynamite, napalm, and other deadly items dropped from the sky did kill an enormous number of human beings. One night, for example, the United States burned at least 83,000 people in Tokyo by scattering fire bombs across that city. An earlier raid in Europe, orchestrated by Sir Arthur Harris, scorched and otherwise killed 42,000 in Hamburg. And at Dresden—*Ah! Dresden!*—some 2,372 bombers managed in one night to destroy approximately fifty people apiece. But the infantry was nevertheless necessary to defeat both the Japanese and the Germans. And in that so-called clean air war, Britain alone lost 72,530 men, most of them brave and skilled: *more than all the officers killed in World War I.*

Much later, the bishops of air power would claim that their acolytes won the war against Japan. Their massive fire raids, culminating in the two atomic bombs, converted many of the heathen. Forgotten in the worshiping of the fire ball are the infantrymen who acquired the real estate for the runways close enough for the airplanes to reach Tokyo, Hiroshima, and Nagasaki. And there were some ordinary seamen connected with all that; the boatswains who jammed the landing craft up on the beach and held them there until the infantrymen dug in on the beach. Beyond all that, of course, and the truth of it, is that Japan was defeated by American submarines. It was the pig boats, not the Boeing bombers, that cut the nerves, the veins, and the arteries of the Co-Prosperity Sphere. The periscopes, not the bomb-sights, sank the Rising Sun.

No top-rank American military leader made the mistake of embracing the fantasy of air power. Not George C. Marshall. Not Dwight D. Eisenhower. Those two men had the brains and the guts to say simply that it was impossible to win quickly and thoroughly and at low cost without seriously disrupting American society. Let alone without endangering relationships with the Russians. The choice was between mustering and equipping and delivering *at least 125 divisions* in Europe by 1943 *at the latest* or coming in after the Soviets had done most of the dying.

American leaders were back to basics. Either admit that the United States was an empire and pay the costs of empire—moral and pragmatic—or give up empire, or keep on trying to reap the rewards of empire by finessing those who would have to build huge cemeteries for their dead. Understanding that issue, British Prime Minister Winston Churchill was candid. He said publicly that he had no intention of presiding over the demise of the British Empire. Roosevelt was not candid. He had no intention of presiding over the end of the American Empire, but he talked about freedom while he gambled on winning the war quickly and completely without upsetting the American people.

So he settled in to finesse the Russians. In the military sense that ploy took the form of limiting the Army to ninety divisions. Marshall and Eisenhower recognized the grave moral and pragmatic risks involved. If the United States did not do all it could as quickly as possible to aid the Red Army, an avowed and necessary ally, then it would forfeit confidence and trust. And if it did not do all that it could to help destroy the enemy, then it would weaken its position at the peace table—and in subsequent postwar negotiations and relationships. Unless it paid the price for—or changed—its imperial way of life, America would inevitably face another crisis after World War II. *At the time, on July 28, 1942, Eisenhower thought that the decision against an early second front in France might well come to be known as the* "blackest day in history."

Roosevelt's disingenuousness had by then sowed dragon's teeth in the relationship with Russia. Using his personal charm, and other sly skills, he had several months earlier led the Soviets to believe that a cross-Channel invasion would occur in 1942. One can understand the President's confidence in his abilities. After all, he had outmaneuvered some very astute politicians at home—and elsewhere. But misleading the Russians involved trying to fox not a chicken, not even a raccoon, but a bear.

It is often said that nothing would have established a relationship of trust with the Soviets. Not only were they congenitally paranoid, so runs the argument, but they were also bent on world conquest. We do know, however, that Russian leaders disagreed among themselves about relations with the United States. Hence a policy of candor and sustained effort to aid the Soviets might well have produced positive results. We can very probably gain more insight into the nature and consequences of Roosevelt's approach by considering two quite different situations separated in place and time.

One concerns the estimate of American policy later made by French leader Charles de Gaulle. The Grand General, as he preferred to be called, understood the strategy and tactics of the finesse as well as Roosevelt. And, far better than most subsequent American leaders, de Gaulle knew that the United States was an empire, and he accepted that fact of life. During World War II, and perhaps for a time afterward, it seems likely that he was deeply resentful of that truth: France was being displaced by an upstart. Over the years, however, the General came to understand that the danger was not primarily in the fact of empire but in its nature and in the unwillingness of the United States to admit to being an empire. And so he undertook to protect France against the consequences of that fundamental irresponsibility. Thus the central point: *if de Gaulle had been in power in Russia the results would have been very similar*. He would have made the same kind of effort to avoid becoming an *object* of American diplomacy, and would have struggled vigorously to gain acceptance as an equal.

The other illuminating episode occurred in Washington about a year before Roosevelt's disingenuous conversations with the Russians about an early second front in Europe. Whatever the rhetoric of the New Deal, the President had never done anything of consequence to help American blacks (or any other people with colored skins). And so in January 1941, their most militant and impressive leader, A. Philip

Randolph, began to organize a massive march on Washington "to exact their rights" as part of a war that he knew would be presented as a war in the name of freedom.

Roosevelt ignored the early news about the project. Then he backed and filled. He *was* a master of the dilly-dally that distracted and enervated many critics or opponents. He fiddled and faddled for six months. Finally, in the summer of 1941, he finessed the crisis by issuing an Executive Order (No. 8802) that ostensibly ended discrimination—if not racism—against blacks in war industries and the federal bureaucracy (including the military). The President did not, however, impose or execute any penalties for failure to comply. He did not say that there would be no contracts for corporations which failed forthwith to hire a consequential number of blacks and treat them equitably. He did not announce that labor unions which refused to enroll a meaningful number of blacks would be denied certification as legitimate bargaining agents. No matter, the blacks backed off. The master had won again. But in time it would become apparent that he and his successors were too clever by half. They out-foxed themselves.

The Russians were not American blacks. They wanted American troops hunkered down in French hedgerows. Now. And if they were not there the Red Army would move westward beyond its own borders *in the process of destroying the German army*. Roosevelt defused a march in Washington at little or no cost to his corporate coalition, but he undermined his relationship with the Soviets. And he trapped himself. Victory by the Red Army was the key to avoiding any structural changes at home.

II

There is no mystery about any of it. The strategy was to use the Soviets to sustain a capitalist political economy. And it worked, at least for a time. It finessed the Russians in the short run, but it benumbed the American citizen. Of course some people died. But one of the most revealing bits of information about the history of America's part in World War II is that it is surprisingly difficult to find a simple statement of how many Americans died in the conflict. We seem to prefer to slide away, drop off, from that truth. But, if you persist, you can find it tucked away under the heading of "Selected Characteristics of the Armed Forces by War" near the back of the *Historical Statistics of the United States*. The number is 405,399.

That *is* a lot of gold stars on the window instead of on the report card. And many very unhappy people—living as well as dead. But with equal truth it is a small price to pay for empire as a way of life. *If you accept, that is to say, the truth that empire is your way of life.* Otherwise, of course, it seems exorbitant. Even maybe irresponsible. After all, empire is our Manifest Destiny. The American imperial way of life conditions people to be outraged about the death required to sustain the empire. It is Alice in Wonderland brought back through the mirror as reality.

On the face of it, say as an exercise in double-entry book-keeping, and assuming the absolute worst about other people's motives or objectives, the Rooseveltian finesse looks rather good. We did win the war cheaply. The Soviets, for example, lost at least 20 *million* human beings. Nobody knows how many Chinese died. Measured against our 405,399, we emerge as the most efficient war machine of all time. All of which is to say that the atom bomb was not a *moral* turning point, simply a *pragmatic* breakthrough. We refined the cost efficiency of killing beyond the imagination of anyone anywhere—in geography or in time.

But the problem was that Americans had become accustomed to winning without paying any significant costs. It was like the game of Truth and Consequences without any

Consequences. The Russians and the Chinese supplied the capital, and we busted the bank. While the Russians lost 20 million lives, for example, the United States created 17 million new jobs safe from bombs or bullets.

Those workers, including large numbers of women and teenagers—even some blacks and browns—sometimes had trouble finding places to live or other substantial ways to invest their money. As a result, the entertainment industry boomed. It was more than a bit like prohibition in the 1920s: save the lives to waste the lives. As one bureaucratic wit remarked, "Americans are finding fun—and liking it." At the moment of the ostensibly greatest sacrifice, in 1944, the total of goods and services available to American citizens outside the armed forces was greater than it had been in 1936.

Roosevelt could not suppress a smile. Surely, he remarked, " 'sacrifice' is not exactly the proper word to describe this program of self-denial." Face it: the vast majority of Americans fought the war in perfect safety and comfort, though perhaps not in luxury. They had never in their immediate memory had it so good. Let there be no doubt. When it is going well, empire as a way of life is a smashing success. Not only no depression, but all kinds of goodies on the table and all kinds of intellectual and psychological yum-yums to be savored and devoured. As Stalin remarked, "things are not that bad in the United States."

The Saturday Evening Post agreed. Writing vintage science-fiction, truly marvelous imaginative nonsense illustrated by that master of romantic realism Norman Rockwell, the editors defined America as "the last bulwark of civilization" created by "Free Enterprise." Thomas Jefferson's best hope crowned as the ultimate truth. "We Americans can boast that we are not as other men are." The only trouble, as one close adviser warned Roosevelt, was that "seven out of ten expect to be personally worse off after the war." Those people did not have all that much confidence in the system. So the experts warned the President: "This feeling that even the winning of the war may bring economic disaster presents a storm warning."

It was indeed disturbing, particularly when at least seven out of ten policy-makers shared the fears of the ordinary folk. As those people formulated it, the choice was not simple, but it was clear. Give up the idea of global empire or go for broke. "We ought to have our cake and eat it too; that we ought to be free to operate under this regional arrangement [the exclusive Monroe Doctrine] and at the same time intervene promptly in Europe." So spoke John McCloy, intimate adviser to Secretary of War Stimson. Or listen to still another Rockefeller, this time Nelson: we must control Latin America to "do what we wanted to do on the world front." So much for the argument that regional settlements were anti-imperial.

The citizenry was sent off to Limbo, that marvelous country of the powerless. Domestic breakdown followed by international crises left them at the mercy of their ostensible leaders. They were offered what appeared to be a choice, but it was so distorted as to be no more than a cruelly sophisticated version of that old tease about have you stopped beating your wife. Do you favor empire as a way of life and the continuation of your present freedom and prosperity, or do you prefer to honor your avowed ideals and risk a depression? It was not an honest question but it was highly effective politics.

III

Roosevelt was in a double bind. His strategy of winning at the least possible cost and disruption had created a false prosperity at home. One of his advisers put it very neatly: "The American people are in the pleasant predicament of having to learn to live 50 percent better than they have ever lived."

Putting all that at risk by limiting the empire raised the prospect of political and social unrest. But the President's military strategy left him with the choice of confronting the Russians or modifying America's imperial way of life.

Politics as the art of the possible had become the necessity of sustaining the empire. Perhaps Roosevelt understood that he had finessed himself. When he told a confidant, shortly before he died, that "we can't do business with Stalin," he was in effect saying that the Russians were neither able nor willing to give the Americans all they wanted without a *quid pro quo*. Their strategic claims were as valid as those of the United States, their economy was extensively and severely damaged, and (as a State Department expert commented) "the emotional and physical exhaustion of the Soviet masses" posed a serious political problem for Russian leaders.

Roosevelt had gambled on a ninety-division army and he had lost. At great cost, the men in the line managed to stop the German 1944 counteroffensive in the Ardennes, at the Battle of the Bulge, but they needed six weeks to resume the offensive. That guaranteed that the Red Army would penetrate deeply into Central Europe. The President was in the position of having to negotiate with people to whom he had lied about a Second Front. Unlike American blacks, the Russians were going to make sure that they secured what they considered their minimum rights and benefits. The only possible way to avoid a frontal confrontation was to be scrupulously honest and open in dealing with the Soviets, moderate America's grandiose expectations and objectives, and negotiate a clear delineation of spheres of interest that involved some kind of economic aid to the Russians. But, even before he died, Roosevelt's handling of the surrender of Italy raised new suspicions in Moscow.

Historians have invested far too much time and energy arguing over the importance of Roosevelt's death. It made very little difference. That judgment does not hinge on quotations from his last days: it instead comes down to a big issue and a symbolic act. There is *no* hard evidence that Roosevelt intended to deploy his charisma and his political savvy to challenge, even to modify, the imperial way of life that he and other Americans had accepted and internalized as The Truth. And it was Roosevelt who removed Vice President Henry A. Wallace from consequential power long before Harry S Truman sent Wallace back to Iowa.

Professor Blum is surely right about that: Roosevelt's dropping Wallace as Vice-President tells us all we need to know about the limits of American liberalism and the nature of its internationalism. The limits were imperial. Even the idea of a regional, perhaps even relaxed, empire proved too much for Roosevelt and other policy-makers to consider—let alone accept and put into operation.

The President dumped Wallace because of the rising opposition among liberals as well as conservatives to any significant modification of the traditional American outlook. But Wallace himself reveals how far the grounds of debate had been narrowed by the experiences and effects of the depression and the war. He wanted little more than for the United States to be *truly* benevolent and progressive in exercising its imperial power. He made his strongest point in a July 1946 letter to President Harry S Truman. Viewed from abroad, American policy appeared to indicate that we "are trying to build up a predominance of force to intimidate the rest of mankind."

Wallace wanted to concentrate less on the Russians and more on building a *good* empire. Chester Bowles said very similar things but in the end gave away his argument by appealing to the lowest common denominator of empire: "*more* for everybody." A few others, largely within the government, made stronger arguments. Herbert Hoover, for example, told Truman to relax—"hold up our banner of what we thought was right and let it go at that"—and concentrate on developing a viable hemispheric political economy.

Five years later Hoover belatedly went public with that approach. He might not have been heeded even in 1944–45, largely because Roosevelt and other Democrats had destroyed his credibility, but by 1950 he had no chance. He was in the position of a father of the 1960s trying to persuade his children that the jazz of the 1920s and 1930s was worth a good listen and a good boogie.

Others, even including Secretary of War Stimson, suggested that the atomic bomb made it imperative to redefine empire in less than global terms. Such people argued a rational case: accept some limits and get on with the labor of sustaining American development within that framework. It was not an anti-imperial outlook; but it did bespeak a knowing, as Walter Lippmann put it, that "we have come to the end of our effortless security and of our limitless opportunity."

Truman had no sympathy with Wallace, and was coolly indifferent to Stimson, Hoover, and other spokesmen of their approach. When Wallace tried to take the debate to the public in a 1948 third party campaign, moreover, Truman had no hesitation in smearing him as a dangerous radical—if not worse. Other politicians perfected that technique of avoiding a serious debate with critics by calling them spokesmen for the enemy, but Truman deserves a considerable measure of credit for showing that it was effective. Effective political power had become ever more narrowly concentrated in the alliance of economic giants and the government that had been created during the depression and the war. The power of the citizen had been reduced to saying yes or no to choices defined and presented by others, or to agitating for essentially secondary benefits within the imperial way of life.

Truman's basic outlook was clearly revealed during a cabinet meeting in September 1945. After listening to the President expound at length on the subject, one cabinet member asked him why it was necessary for the United States to "police the world." Truman was courteous but clearly impatient. It had to be done, he explained, with two references to the frontier era of American history: "in order to carry out a just decision the court must have marshals"; and "in order to collect monies for county governments it has been found necessary to employ a sheriff." The implications of those homey analogies are as staggering as they are illuminating. The United States was at once the just judge (and jury), the center of global government, and the marshal or policeman enforcing that power.

Whatever literary polish was lacking in Truman's folksy idiom, the President's Wilsonianism shone through in all its global splendor. And Truman, like Wilson, could talk about the nuts and bolts of the political economy. A large volume of trade in exports and raw materials (and related financial arrangements) was necessary "to achieve prosperity in the United States." It thus followed that "peace, freedom, and world trade—are inseparable."

The President was also impatient for results. One moment captures it all. At the Potsdam Conference in 1945, exhilarated by the news that the atomic bomb worked, he revealed his frustrations with the serious labor of negotiations with the Russians. It was not even so much that Stalin kept insisting on explicit agreements. It was simply that Truman wanted to get on with imperial matters. American imperial matters. He said it all to his Secretary of State James F. Byrnes: "Jimmy, do you realize that we have been here seventeen whole days. Why, in seventeen days you can decide anything."*

---

* Some accounts of this episode report that Truman said *ten* days; but I am willing to give the President the benefit of the doubt.

As with a good many southern politicians of his generation, Byrnes could also say it very neatly. He expressed the central thrust of America's imperial policy with considerable flair early in 1946. "We must help our friends in every way and refrain from assisting those who either through helplessness or for other reasons are opposing the principles for which we stand."*

But many people revealed a talent for the pithy sentence in the service of the imperial way of life. The ultimate reduction to nonsense was offered by Henry B. Luce, master in residence of *Time, Life,* and various other corporate enterprises. In a truly classic essay, he defined it all as "The American Century." Luce was a deeply religious man who was inclined to think of the Second Coming as the day when China and the United States did unto others as they desired. But Luce was broad-minded, and so he opened the pages of *Life* to another priest named Reinhold Niebuhr. Niebuhr was the most sought-after soul-sitter for American liberalism. "For peace we must risk war. . . . We will have to stand at every point in our far-flung lines."

John Foster Dulles and John Fitzgerald Kennedy, among others, later embroidered those lines with their own intellectual needlework. Perhaps more properly, their piecework. Luce and Niebuhr did it freehand, from the soul, while their successors (whatever their craft) were at most improvising on the printed pattern. Except again those fascinating southerners. Let me put it this way. Lincoln won the Civil War, but his Faustian bargain left us with southerners doing their cotton-picking best to catch up with northerners who were being tough and successful.

---

*Dean G. Acheson later refined this to read: "We are willing to help people who believe the way we do, to continue to live the way they want to live." I suppose the difference is explained by the necessity for southerners, who lost the Civil War, to express themselves with a mite more discretion. On the other hand, Byrnes may have had the better of it by any accounting.

Here we can usefully juxtapose Theodore Roosevelt and Thomas Terry Connally. Roosevelt defined the Open Door Policy as nothing more than the projection of the Monroe Doctrine westward to Asia. Connally, by 1945 the master of the United States Senate, slyly shot the arrow east. The military alliance between America and western European nations against the Soviet Union "is but the logical extension of the principle of the Monroe Doctrine." After all those years, the South was reintegrated as part of the empire.

Still and all, we need to know whether or not such public breast-beating is indeed the outward expression of private conviction. Here the crucial documents involve the response within the government (now for all purposes The State) to an extremely long cable sent early in 1946 by a bureaucrat named George Frost Kennan in Moscow to his superiors in Washington. However much it has been analyzed and explained, even by Kennan himself (particularly by Kennan), it remains the hinge of policy.

Kennan later claimed that his analysis of Soviet behavior and his policy recommendations had been misunderstood and misapplied. There is some justification for that complaint, but it does not speak to the principal issue. Kennan chose to fight his battles inside the government, and his early public statement of his views can hardly be called subtle. He described the Soviet Union in crude mechanical metaphors (wind-up toys that stop only when they run into walls); and promised that such containment would subvert and replace the existing government and system.

One hardly needs to speculate about how the Russians responded to Kennan's views, or to his prompt and extensive influence among American leaders. After all, Stalin and his advisers were subtle enough to understand the imperial nature of the Open Door Policy. Stalin viewed it as being "as dangerous to a nation as foreign military invasion." So to be told publicly, in *Foreign Affairs*, that he was an evil wind-up toy was hardly calculated to promote a relaxation of tensions. Kennan *did* approve the article as published. And by then, 1947, he was quite aware that his hyperventilated rhetoric had been embraced by his superiors as the first and only commandment.

In a broader sense, Kennan typified the fundamentally non-democratic attitude and outlook of the inner circle of American policy-makers. He and his peers were wholly persuaded that the public lacked either the intelligence or experience required to formulate or conduct foreign policy. That is why he never took his case to the public. He was an elitist who stuck with the elite. If, as he came to disagree with the hard-liners like Secretary of State Dean Acheson, he had gone public he might well have helped others like Walter Lippmann to create an informed and consequential criticism that could have saved America much anguish, pain, and death.

As it happened, Acheson never had to engage Kennan in an ongoing public dialogue. He could file him and forget him. For that matter, Kennan's increasing skepticism probably intensified Acheson's overriding fear of the economic, social, and political "*disintegration*" of the capitalist political economy. One astute observer who talked a good bit with Acheson came away with this estimate: the Secretary thought "that, in the final analysis, the United States was the locomotive at the head of mankind, and the rest of the world the caboose." A sympathetic biographer used remarkably similar terms: Acheson believed that "only the United States had the power to grab hold of history and make it conform."

The answer to the question—conform to what?—was never in doubt. Conform to the image of the world provided by the American imperial way of life. Senator Arthur H. Vandenberg, who was never charged with being soft toward the Russians, made the point this way. After a discussion with Acheson about a projected conference with the Soviets, the Senator offered this private assessment to a friend. Acheson "is so totally anti-Soviet and is going to be so *completely* tough that I really doubt whether there is any *chance at all*" for compromise or agreement.

What Truman, Acheson, and others took from Kennan was the stark reformulation of Lincoln's strategy of containment. What Kennan said between 1945 and 1948 was what Lincoln had said between 1848 and 1861: put a wall around the Russians (the South) and that evil society will disintegrate. Whatever their reputations as students of history, neither Truman nor Acheson paid any heed to the *known*— let alone the unknown—costs of Lincoln's strategy when put to the test.

Nor were they responsive to any indications that the Soviets were interested in an accommodation between the two empires. It appears highly probable, indeed almost certain, that Stalin was seeking that kind of arrangement in 1949; a sort of imperial live and let live in place of global communism or a global open door. It was bluntly imperial, but it was honest, and it did offer everyone a chance to assign first priority to domestic objectives and programs.

The world looked relatively manageable in late summer 1949. The United States had won in Iran, the Soviets in Czechoslovakia. America controlled the Middle East, most particularly the oil in Saudi Arabia, and enjoyed as its allies the reinvigorated and modernized workshops in Germany and Japan. In addition the Russians had been held at bay in Yugoslavia and Berlin. A thoughtful and responsible imperial elite would not have been particularly upset by the *overall* meaning of various events that occurred during the autumn.

American leaders behaved differently. First in China, where a corrupt and disreputable government gave over in disgrace to quasi-puritanical communist revolutionaries led by Mao Tse-tung. Mao immediately asked to open serious discussions with the United States. Truman and Acheson would have none of it, denying American officials permission *even to talk* with Mao and refused to recognize his government. Mao was indicating, with the approval of his party's Executive Committee, that he wanted to explore the possibility of becoming a Tito, of developing a socialist but independent China. In their wisdom, Truman and Acheson defined Mao as a puppet of Stalin.

Almost simultaneously, the Russians tested a nuclear device. That meant that *sometime in the future* they could make and deliver such a bomb. Very shortly after the successful test explosion, with Stalin firmly in residence in the Kremlin, two of his most interesting subalterns—Georgi Malenkov and Nikita Khrushchev—began to speculate in public about using the stand-off to prove that socialism could create a better society than capitalism under conditions of peaceful competition. They were in effect saying that we now feel relatively secure. You have your empire, we have ours. Let us see who does the most effective and impressive job of creating the good imperial society.

Instead, Truman and Acheson ordered a crash program to produce an even more monstrous bomb, and set a task force to work to project the containment strategy to its ultimate conclusion as the basis for American policy. The result was the most impressive statement of the assumptions, ethos, and pragmatics of empire as a way of life ever generated and approved by the government of the United States. By comparison, for example, Henry Luce's sermon about The American Century seems like a grandfatherly talk by Billy Graham to Sunday schoolers on a picnic. There are many imperial documents tucked away in the archives, but National Security Council Document No. 68, dated April 14, 1950, is one of the most awesome.

The context of the document involves far more than the

nuclear device tested by the Soviets.* Let us begin with the military base line as defined by two factors. First, as several times noted in NSC-68, the United States enjoyed the capacity "to deliver a serious [nuclear] blow against the war-making capacity of the U.S.S.R." That power was considered adequate "to deter the Kremlin from a deliberate direct military attack against ourselves or other free peoples." Second, the Soviet lack of any comparable stock of bombs or an effective delivery system meant that American leaders were dealing with the possibility of a future change in that situation, not with an existing condition of parity.

American leaders were well aware, moreover, that Winston Churchill had been arguing since 1947 that the United States and its allies should use that monopoly of nuclear weapons to enter into serious negotiations with the Russians to "bring matters to a head and make a final settlement." The signals from Malenkov and Khrushchev underscored that advice, as did recommendations from various people within the United States, West Germany, and France. Perhaps George Kennan was the most significant figure in that group, if only because he had become ever more concerned about the militarization of his policy of containment.

But the policy review group, established on Truman's order as a "matter of urgency," began its deliberations on precisely that basis. Their key reference document was National Security Council Document 20/4 of November 24, 1948, which called for a build-up of power to create divisions among the peoples of the Soviet Union and "bring about a basic change in the conduct" of the Kremlin. Hence in 1950 the kind of negotiations that Churchill was recommending were ruled out save as "only a tactic" until a massive increase in military spending made it possible to apply the pressure

*I am indebted here, and in the following chapter, to suggestions by Sheldon Meyer; and to several discussions with Edward Crapol.

required "to compel the acceptance of terms consistent with our objectives."

Here it is crucial to understand what American leaders meant by that phrase "our objectives." As stated by them several times, it was to build an international order "harmonious with our fundamental national purposes," a "world environment in which the American system can survive and flourish." That almost palpable concern for global order and security is apparent throughout the long document, and is expressed most dramatically in two striking passages.

First, the analysis and policy recommendations are presented in the context of the breakdown of the 19th-century imperial systems. Wars and revolutions, noted NSC-68 on the first page, led to the collapse of five empires—the Ottoman, the German, the Austro-Hungarian, the Italian, and the Japanese—and the "drastic decline" of the French and British empires; as well as to unrest and turmoil in the areas formerly controlled by those powers. The United States must establish a new order to replace the old. Second, that general imperial responsibility was dramatized by this remarkable comment: *"Even if there were no Soviet Union we would face the great problem . . . [that] the absence of order among nations is becoming less and less tolerable."* *

Only then is the problem discussed in terms of the Soviet Union. While its capabilities "are inferior to those of our Allies and to our own," and its society riddled with "rot," it must nevertheless become the focus of the effort to create "a successfully functioning political and economic system." Hence it was "not an adequate objective merely to check the Kremlin" because that would not be enough to establish and guarantee the new global order. (So much for Churchill.)

The only solution was to "foster a fundamental change in the nature of the Soviet system"; "foster the seeds of destruc-

* Italics added.

tion within the Soviet system"; force it to "change its policies drastically." The basic strategy was thus developed "with a view to fomenting and supporting unrest and revolt in selected strategic satellite countries," and "to reduce the power and influence of the Kremlin inside the Soviet Union." That would create a situation "in which the Russian peoples will have a new chance to work out their own destiny."

The tactics involved "any means, covert or overt, violent or non-violent." Those included "overt psychological warfare," covert "economic warfare," superficial negotiations as part of presenting the policy as "essentially defensive" in character, and major increases in all categories of military spending. The latter would of necessity require increasing taxes while reducing appropriations for domestic programs. But, pointing to the experience of World War II, the authors of NSC-68 confidently predicted that the increase in military spending would prevent the possibility of any socially and politically explosive "real decrease in the standard of living." Once again, guns *and* butter.

Unquestionably, NSC-68 is one of the truly impressive imperial documents in the long tradition of the Western European expansion around the world. Its creation and adoption by the leaders of a society that was founded on the Declaration of Independence is mysterious or paradoxical only if one forgets John Locke and Thomas Jefferson. Remember, for example, that Locke's essays on liberty and freedom were integrated with his definition of wealth as "having more than the rest of the world." And recall that Jefferson, who wrote the Declaration, owned slaves and was ambivalent about whether or not the First Americans were truly human. And that his strategy for dealing with neighbors he considered troublesome—"the only way of preventing" such difficulties—was to conquer Florida and Canada.

No one has commented more succinctly than Professor Weinberg. "Again and again . . . one experiences the same

difficulty in understanding why particular actions and policies were subsumed under the doctrine of self-defense." And
why Americans considered themselves, in a state of "hysterical apprehensiveness," as having a "preordained right to *ideal*
security"—now and on into the future. Yet that is precisely
what NSC-68 sought in a wholly imperial framework. It
provides the benchmark for understanding American foreign
policy from April 1950 down to our own time.

CHAPTER NINE
The Empire at Bay

We are the most ambitious people the world has ever seen:— & I greatly fear we shall sacrifice our liberties to our imperial dreams.

HENRY J. RAYMOND, editor of the *New York Times*,
to SECRETARY OF STATE WILLIAM SEWARD, 1864

Our frontiers today are on every continent.

JOHN FITZGERALD KENNEDY, 1960

No single nation however big and powerful can dominate a world of some 140 interdependent nations and embracing some four billion people.

R. S. RAJARATAN,
Singapore Minister of Foreign Affairs, 1979

IN A RARE moment of candor, Acheson admitted in 1953 that he and Truman might not have been able to sustain their grandiose imperial policy if the North Koreans had not "come along and saved us." Actually, Acheson did not even say "North Koreans." He said "Korea." Given his reputation for sometimes shading the truth so finely as to render it indistinguishable from an ordinary lie, that remark prompted some observers to reopen the question of whether or not South Korea, with the overt or tacit approval of the United States, provoked the North Korean attack of June 1950.

On balance, however, it was simply one of those wars that anybody could have counted on to erupt some time. Both halves of that divided country were dying to start dying to unite themselves. That old deb'l nationalism raised to fever pitch by very strong shots of mutually exclusive theologies. In any event, the debate about who bears ultimate responsibility obscures the fundamental issue of the response by Truman and Acheson.

Clearly, when the Secretary acknowledged that Korea "saved us," he did not mean in the sense of preventing the defeat or the destruction of the United States. He meant only that it allowed the government to implement the apocalyptic imperial strategy of NSC-68. Primed and ready, armed (or driven) psychologically as well as with the heady rhetoric of that document, they simply went to war. They by-passed the Congress and the public and confronted both with an accomplished fact. A few phone calls, and it was done. Go to bed at peace and wake up at war.

It was even more dramatic than the subsequent intervention in Vietnam as a demonstration of the centralization of power inherent in empire as a way of life. The State had literally been compressed or consolidated into the President and his like-minded appointees. In a marvelously revealing description, underscoring Truman's earlier lecture to the cabinet, the war without a declaration of war was called a "police action." Ironically, the most succinct commentary on Truman's remark was provided by the editor of the *New York Times*. "We are the most ambitious people the world has ever seen," noted Henry J. Raymond on May 30, 1864, "— & I greatly fear we shall sacrifice our liberties to our imperial dreams."

I

The military containment and subsequent rout of North Korean forces (by the end of September 1950) created a moment of imperial euphoria. American leaders were high on NSC-68. The United States undertook to liberate North Korea by conquest and integrate it into the American Empire. It was assumed in Washington that such action would accelerate the process of disintegration within and between Russia and China and so finally create an open door world. Then came the moment of truth, and the empire suddenly found itself at bay. The Chinese entered the war with massive force on October 26 and drove the Americans southward to the line that originally divided Korea.

Once again one thinks of the way American leaders failed to comprehend the willingness of black citizens to settle for promises of future equality and freedom at home. They had first misread and misapplied that episode in their dealings with the Russians; then with the Chinese; and finally, with increasing frequency, in Latin America, Africa, Southeast Asia, and the Middle East. The mistaken assumption that other poor and demeaned peoples would display similar forbearance appeared as the cosmic cost of such prejudice and racism.

The Roosevelts, the Trumans and the Achesons, and most of their successors, fundamentally misconceived the deeply patriotic—even loving—commitment of American blacks to what Martin Luther King called The Dream of America. And because they could not acknowledge the existence of an American Empire, they could not comprehend—let alone understand—that other so-called inferiors felt the same love for their cultures; and that, viewing America as an empire which threatened the integrity and existence of their cultures, they would ultimately fight rather than accept indirect destruction.

The empire had been brought to bay. Dwight David Eisenhower understood that essential truth, and further realized that the future character of American society depended upon how the culture responded. His first objective after he became President in 1952 was to end the Korean police action before it spiraled into World War III. That accomplished, he set about to calm Americans, cool them off, and refocus their attention and energies on domestic development. He was a far more perceptive and cagey leader than many people realized at the time—or later.

The image of a rather absent-minded, sometimes bumbling if not incoherent Uncle Ike was largely his own shrewd cover for his serious efforts to get control of the military (and other militant cold warriors), to decrease tension with Russia, and somehow begin to deal with the fundamental distortions of American society. He clearly understood that crusading imperial police actions were extremely dangerous, and he was determined to avoid World War III. When Britain, France, and Israel attacked Egypt in 1956 over the nationalization of the Suez Canal, the President called British Prime Minister Anthony Eden and scolded him sharply: "Anthony, you must have gone out of your mind."

When the moment came, Eisenhower could be just as blunt with Americans. A good many of them were probably shocked when, in his farewell address of 1961, he spoke candidly and forcefully about the military-industrial complex that since 1939 had become the axis of the American political economy. That was such a catchy phrase that not many of them noticed that he went on to assault the distortion of education involved in that consolidation of power. The historically free and critical university, he noted, "the fountainhead of free ideas and scientific discovery, has experienced a revolution in the conduct of research. . . . A governmental contract becomes virtually a substitute for intellectual curiosity."

The speech was not an aberration: Eisenhower had become ever more deeply concerned with those issues after retiring from the army. Thus, while it is true that he was not an intellectual, and was conservative in many ways, it is also true that he had a firm sense of how The State had gradually taken over the very process of creating and controlling basic ideas—the ways of making sense of reality. Or, in a different way, how The State used its extensive control of information, and its ability to make major decisions in the name of security, to create an ideology ever more defined in content as well as rhetoric as an imperial way of life.

Eisenhower's most serious weakness did not lie in his fidelity to a rudimentary version of marketplace economics, or even in his excessive caution about how quickly and how far he could move the American citizenry away from its imperial

obsessions with Russia, China, and other revolutionary movements. It was defined instead by his unwillingness to translate
his valid perceptions into strong policies and active sustained
leadership. He lacked Hoover's (let alone Churchill's)
toughness about accepting the limits of American power, and
the former President's knowledge that the only way to deal
with the costly and unhealthy consequences of empire was to
begin creating a different way of life. Given his charisma,
Eisenhower could have initiated that process and perhaps
even created an irreversible momentum.

Failing to do that, he left no dynamic legacy. The militant
advocates of the global imperial way of life quickly reasserted
their power and policy. They, too, recognized that the Chinese counter-intervention in Korea had brought the empire
to a critical juncture. Their response was to reassert American power and get on with policing the world in the name of
benevolent progress. Led by John Fitzgerald Kennedy, and
calling themselves the New Frontiersmen, they perfectly expressed the psychopathology of the empire at bay and its
consequences. Onward and outward in the spirit of NSC-68.
"Ask not what your country can do for you," intoned Kennedy in his 1961 inaugural address, "ask what you can do for
your country." By country, of course, they meant *their* government.

Kennedy and his advisers had the brilliant perception to
talk about the empire in the classic idiom of the frontier.
That propaganda gem is of itself almost enough to justify
honoring them as the cleverest imperial leaders of their generation. The best that Henry Kissinger could do a few years
later, for example, was to blurt out a crude reference to the
same idiom—presenting himself as Gary Cooper in *High
Noon*. The excessively self-conscious Dr. Cowboy will ride
on stage in good time, but for the moment let us concentrate
on those Kennedy hands who were born and bred to empire.

"Our frontiers today," cried Kennedy, "are on every continent." America has "obligations," he explained, "which stretch ten thousand miles across the Pacific, and three and four thousand miles across the Atlantic, and thousands of miles to the south. Only the United States—and we are only six percent of the world's population—bears this kind of burden." He understandably neglected to mention that the burden on the metropolis was somewhat eased by the benefits of controlling a grossly disproportionate percentage of the world's resources. He was more concerned to create the psychological mood of impending doom: "The tide of events has been running out and time has not been our friend."

The failure of the effort early in 1961 to overthrow Fidel Castro's revolution in Cuba intensified that trauma. Not only did the rhetoric become ever more apocalyptic ("this time of maximum danger"), but Kennedy immediately began a massive military build-up in the spirit of NSC-68 (three special requests for extra funds during 1961). Then he indulged himself in a truly arrogant and irresponsible act. Knowing that the United States enjoyed a massive superiority in strategic weapons, Kennedy publicly goaded, even insulted, the Soviet Union by gloating about its gross inferiority.

He scared the Russians viscerally; and in the process not only prompted them to launch a desperate effort to correct the vast imbalance, but very probably touched-off the internal Soviet dialogue that led to the confrontation in 1962 over Russian missiles in Cuba. The more evidence that appears about that moment on the edge of the abyss, the more it seems probable that the Soviets never had any intention of going to war. Taken with all appropriate skepticism, for example, Premier Nikita Khrushchev's account very likely contains the essence of the truth: Moscow was less concerned with the possibility of a second invasion of Cuba than with somehow—even at sizable risk—jarring Washington into a realization that, if pushed to the wall, the Russians would fight rather than surrender. Given their grave inferiority, the only way they could make that point was by creating a situation that would dramatize for Americans the threat as experienced daily by the Soviets.

Kennedy's understanding of that message was limited. He spoke of the need to avoid further such crises, but he clearly felt that America had regained the initiative; that he was now free to deploy American forces to prevent or control further change that might weaken the American empire. He did talk about accepting diversity among the poor and developing nations, and about programs to facilitate some social and economic improvements in Latin America and other countries. And he did make some efforts, as in the Alliance for Progress and the Peace Corps, to act on that rhetoric. But he also embarked upon an obsessive campaign to murder Castro, and he deployed between 15,000 and 20,000 American troops (many of them in the field as advisers) to intervene in the revolutionary civil war in Vietnam. Those frontiers on every continent were going to remain frontiers in the traditional American meaning of a frontier—a region to penetrate and control and police and civilize.

II

This essay, an effort to review our development as an empire and to encourage a searching dialogue among ourselves about the character of our culture, has never attempted to offer a detailed reconstruction of American foreign policy. Hence it would be a contradiction in terms to wander off into a blow-by-blow account of recent events. But it does seem useful to explore some of the contemporary aspects of our imperial way of life.

Let us begin with the relationship between NSC-68 and the civil rights movement of the 1950s and 1960s; and let us assume that American leaders, whatever their prejudices or racism, believed that the empire would provide blacks and other disadvantaged groups (including poor whites) with greater opportunities and rewards. Their most popular euphemism for empire—*growth*—was invoked on the grounds that the same share of an ever larger pie would produce improvement for everyone. And elitists like Acheson had reason to believe that the minorities and other poor would continue to be patient until the fruits of empire were harvested.

But the war in Korea, and the related increase in military spending, revealed the true priorities of the empire and hence dramatized the discrepancy involved in talking about empire in terms of liberty, freedom, equality, and welfare while denying those benefits to large numbers of people at home. That contradiction was further highlighted by the nonviolent nature of black protest against being denied elementary equity on the buses of Montgomery, Alabama, in 1955, and in the eating places of Greensboro, North Carolina, in 1960. Some white Americans recognized and became upset about that contrast, but neither Eisenhower nor Kennedy devised an effective response. The former was socially and politically too conservative and cautious, and the latter was more concerned with standing-up to the Russians all along America's global frontier.

But Lyndon Baines Johnson did make a brave—and in the end tragic—effort to resolve that visceral contradiction in the imperial way of life. He tried to make major improvements in the quality of life for the poor and disadvantaged of all colors (and therefore for all other Americans), and at the same time secure the frontier in Indochina. That proved to be impossible because by 1964–65 the dynamics of empire as a way of life left him no room for maneuver. Given the legacy of prejudice and racism, and the global definition of America's political economy and its security as formulated in NSC-68, Johnson was trying to swim in the sky. But at least he tried.

Stated bluntly, the President could not muster the votes to help the poor at home unless he honored the imperial ethic in Vietnam. He simply did not enjoy the personal and political advantages that enabled Eisenhower to move quietly toward a less grandiose foreign policy. That meant that any effort to make structural reforms at home would provoke a militant reaction around the classic imperial theme of "Who Lost Whatever Wherever?"

Johnson first tried to finesse the war issue. Therein lies the stuff of great drama. A modern Shakespeare might well do it this way: if only Johnson had gone with his instinct as a Southerner to recognize in the Vietcong the American blacks driven to violence, then he might—just might—have begun the process whereby Americans said no to empire and yes to the vision of community. But the imperial North had forever scarred the South. Left it resentful and determined to prove its valor and its equality. There is a great play in that old fear of the South transformed into a recognition of the truth that one either frees the slaves or confronts a rebellion. But the North had failed to learn that lesson during Reconstruction after the Civil War, and so Johnson had no allies to help him redefine the truth of America.

So from finessing the war Johnson moved to lying about the war. His effort to stand firm on the frontier while effecting reforms at home led him to create enormous inflationary pressures within the economy, and to engage in ever more serious self-deception and public dissembling to sustain popular support for the imperial war. In the end, that is to say, Johnson was the victim of the basic fear, so candidly expressed in NSC-68, that America was fundamentally threatened by *any* disorder in the world. (A fear also revealed in the President's intervention in Santo Domingo.)

That fog of trepidation and dread continued to influence the conduct of foreign affairs by President Richard Milhous Nixon and Secretary of State Henry Kissinger. Their bone marrow anxiety provides the key to resolving the apparent paradox in a diplomacy that sought to stabilize relations with the Soviets while simultaneously recognizing the communist government of China, falsifying official records to hide an illegal and devastating expansion of the Vietnamese war into Cambodia, launching an effort to subvert an *elected* socialist government in Chile, and supporting a dictatorship in Iran that was instrumental in raising oil prices.

No one yet knows the precise nature of the relationship between Nixon and Kissinger. But Kissinger could not have functioned as he did without the support of the President. The Secretary of State has provided the most information about the assumptions that underlay their policies, and it seems apparent that they recognized that the grand objective of NSC-68—the subversion of the Soviet Union—was no longer realistic. Kissinger had long agreed with Churchill, for example, that the United States should have negotiated a broad settlement with the Russians in 1947–48, and concluded during the 1950s that American policy had "reached an impasse."

Thus it was necessary to stabilize the existing balance between the two superpowers. The first step on that road, at least in their view, was to assert their power over the bureaucracies in the State Department and other branches of government; a task Kissinger undertook with great relish as an exercise of his own ego in the service of his great man interpretation of history. That done, Kissinger could begin the effort to order and balance the world.

He now and again admitted the impossibility of doing that without a clear conception of a limited American imperial system, and likewise spoke of the importance of justice; but he never provided either the vision or the definition of justice. Indeed, Kissinger had little patience with anyone who was concerned with the character of the world order he invoked so often. In one classic instance, for example, he dismissed such people for "confusing social reform with geopolitics." Yet his favorite word to define geopolitics was "equilibrium"—little more than a fancy synonym for order. As for justice, Kissinger might usefully have remembered the rabbi's wisdom about Deuteronomy 16.20: "Justice, justice shalt thou pursue." Asked why the word justice is repeated, the rabbi explained that it was done to emphasize the necessity of pursuing justice *with* justice.

Given the Nixon-Kissinger willingness to settle for controlling nothing more than the world outside Russia and Eastern Europe, their policy of detente and strategic arms control was a rational first step toward that objective. And it is certainly arguable that their approach to China (despite their tactics of secrecy and shock) was on balance a positive and stabilizing maneuver as long as it was not allowed to become part of a new strategy of containment designed to destabilize the Soviet Union. And that caveat applies to subsequent American leaders as well as to Kissinger and Nixon.

The weaknesses of the Nixon-Kissinger approach became clear in their dealings with the rest of the world. On the one hand, they defined stabilization as allowing the United States to decide what was permissible and impermissible beyond the Soviet sphere. But, on the other hand, they lacked any significant comprehension or understanding of the dynamic, causal inter-relationships between economics, politics, and social affairs within the poor regions of the world, or between the global rich and poor. Hence they mistakenly linked any changes not approved or controlled by the United States to the influence of the Soviets. The unhappy results became most apparent in Cambodia, Chile, and Iran.

The unconstitutional bombing of Cambodia, which clearly did more to destroy the fabric and morale of that society than the incursion of the North Vietnamese which Kissinger used to justify the monstrous act, is in some respects less revealing of their diplomacy than their actions in Chile and Iran.* The American ambassador to Chile began his report on that nation's presidential election of 1970 in these words: "Chile voted *calmly* to have a Marxist-Leninist state, the first nation in the world to make this choice *freely and knowingly.*" † In keeping with the primary responsibility of a foreign service officer, that is an essentially factual report; although adding the term *Leninist* to Marxist has long been the routine ploy used by those in power in America to turn an avowed socialist into a communist pawn of the Kremlin. The ambassador then offered, in a wholly legitimate way, his evaluation of the evidence: it was in his view "a grievous defeat" for the United States.

Kissinger's account of America's subsequent efforts to prevent Salvador Allende from becoming president of Chile, and later to destabilize and subvert his government, is remarkable for its conscious and unconscious revelations about the Nixon-Kissinger conduct of foreign affairs. Before Allende became president, for example, Kissinger presents the man as a doctrinaire communist in the Russian mould. Once Allende becomes President, however, Kissinger talks about the *possibility* that he will *become* such a puppet. In a similar way, the Secretary of State stresses Allende's narrow plurality in 1970 without once noting, even in a footnote, that Allende increased his vote in the next election, which was held in accordance with Chile's Constitution.

All that tells us more than Kissinger intended us to know, but he is even more illuminating when he insists that "our

---

* Although everyone concerned with the Cambodian matter is indebted to William Shawcross, *Sideshow: Kissinger, Nixon and the Destruction of Cambodia* (New York: Simon and Schuster, 1979), it is important to remember that the House of Representatives Judiciary Committee raised and defined the issue during its consideration of the bill of particulars for the impeachment of President Nixon.
† Italics added.

concern with Allende was based on national security, not on economics," and proceeds to emphasize "American interests in the hemisphere." There are three responses. First, Kissinger cannot seriously expect the observer to believe that Washington was worried about the Russians' turning Chile into a base for a strategic—geopolitical—military attack on the United States. Even he admits that the issue had been settled during the Cuban missile crisis; and, for that matter, refined during his tenure in the basement of the White House.

Second, if Kissinger did in truth not consider economic interests as an integral part of national security ("America's interests in the hemisphere"), then one must conclude that he was stunningly obtuse and probably not qualified to be Secretary of State in the world's premier capitalist political economy.* Third, in view of Kissinger's presentation of himself as a realist, he wholly ignores the feasibility of working with an elected socialist government as a hard-headed as well as moral strategy to counter the Soviet appeal in the Third World and to give hope to all democratic reformers in the poor nations. American leaders seem to be limited in their sight to the left by *benevolent* dictators like Tito of Yugoslavia.

The Secretary's performance in dealing with Iran offers support for all those criticisms. Give him his due: he has quietly and cryptically admitted that his comprehension of the relationships between economic, political, and social development was less than sophisticated. Hardly even rudimentary. But that is only part of the explanation of his fail-

---

* It is possible, of course, that Kissinger made his disavowal in the hope of defusing the criticism that economic concerns were involved in the effort to subvert an elected government. If so, his sensitivity to the charge is revealing in its own right; and, in any event, he would have been better advised to be candid to avoid the thought that he was incompetent.

ure in Iran. For it is extremely doubtful that any one nation could control events in the non-Soviet world. Asked for his comment on the matter, Karl Marx would have laughed aloud in the reading room of the British Museum.

Still and all, it is difficult to imagine how anyone of Kissinger's intelligence could combine more errors of perception, understanding, analysis, and policy in dealing with Iran. Neither he nor Nixon exhibited any sense of that nation's history, or even of its intensely religious and nationalistic pride. And they obviously assumed that Iranians had accepted or forgotten that the United States had grossly intervened to control the resources and the government of that country even before overthrowing an elected government in the 1950s.

Given all that, it is not surprising that they embarked upon a policy doomed to failure. In embracing and arming the Shah, in truth a petty despot, they committed America's geopolitical interests to a government guaranteed to generate ever growing internal opposition to its pretensions. And in supporting, even encouraging, the despot to raise the price of oil to pay for his tinkertoy regime they undercut the foundation of the American imperial way of life they sought to preserve.

In the fundamental sense, the Americans held captive in Iran through and beyond the winter of 1979–80 were hostages to the American Empire. Prisoners taken in payment for the United States treating Iran and other weak countries (in that region, but also elsewhere) as vassals laboring at low wages for the welfare of the imperial metropolis. The story goes back far beyond the 1953 coup that put the Shah back on his throne, let alone the intervention at the end of World War II that played a significant part in the intensification of the Cold War. The tale has its origins in the 19th-century penetration of the region by American traders and Christian missionaries, and becomes a major (if neglected) theme of imperial diplomacy with the advent of Zionism and the importance of oil reserves during the 1920s and 1930s.

Our limited sense of History denies us any significant understanding of how trade, religion, oil, and revolution have converged to create a crisis in the Middle East. Simply put, the hostages are centerpieces carefully placed to dramatize our imperial way of life. They were seized to italicize the imperial nature of the American Way of Life. It would be a mistake to dismiss the religious point being documented by that act (the imperial nature of Christian missionaries), but here I would like to concentrate on the distortion of religion known as Zionism and the economics of oil.

The American inability to distinguish the difference between self-determination for a society of Palestinians (of whatever religion) and a geographical area populated exclusively by self-proclaimed pure Zionists may well generate the Apocalypse. Even if it does not, that confusion has already told us all that we should need to know about *any* people confusing themselves with the Lord. One thinks here of Winthrop, Jefferson, and others confusing metaphor with reality. Of not understanding that a metaphor is a cookie when held too long in the hot fist will crumple into disaster. Of coming to believe that the City on the Hill has the right to expect to control the world.

Not at all after all, indeed in the beginning, the Palestinians are surely every bit as qualified as human beings as the Zionists. Leave it at that. One does think here of how we Americans honored the First Americans only after they had lost. It does not take too much imagination to visualize Begin dedicating a graveyard to Arafat, intoning the usual Western pieties. The point is not to damn Begin. The point is to awaken our own conscience. Think of how we have treated our Begins and Arafats. And we, the happy citizens of the empire, respected American blacks only after they committed their imaginative pacific terroristic acts. They went to eat where they had a perfect legal imperial right to eat even if the imperial citizens beat them bloody. They went to church where they had a perfect legal imperial right to worship the God of their choice even if we bombed them taking communion.

Who is the terrorist?

It simply will not do for Zionists to define themselves as the benevolent, progressive policemen of the Middle East. No more than it will do for us to present ourselves in that idiom on the global scene.

And so to oil. The truth of it is that nobody believes us when we talk about oil as if we were socialists committed to internal equity. The world knows that we are imperialists dedicated to controlling all the oil we can funnel into our bellies. Oil is not the primary cause of empire. It is not even the principal definition of contemporary empire. But it is the slickest way we now lie to ourselves about the nature of empire. Let us risk confronting a bit of history.

Americans began to produce oil near Titusville, Pennsylvania, on August 27, 1859. Fifty years later the United States pumped more than the rest of the world combined. The political economy of capitalism shifted away from coal and neglected to explore other sources of energy. There was a short but intense oil scare between 1917 and 1924: a hullabaloo created by the navy shifting to oil-fired turbines, the Mexican Revolution, the boom in automobiles and airplanes, the beginnings of the petrochemical industry, and the struggle for market supremacy (and survival) among American petroleum corporations.

That crisis disappeared in the cloud of confidence puffed up by the finding of new reserves abroad (as in Venezuela), by new discoveries at home (as in Texas), by more efficient exploration and production at home, and—most particularly—by gaining access to the vast reserves in Saudi Arabia and other poor and weak countries in the Middle East. No better example ever of the rewards of empire as a way of life. But make no mistake, we also came to rely on other cheap materials from the provinces.

The United States continued to produce half the world's oil until, in 1948, it became a net *importer* of oil. True imperial dependency upon the natives. But that phrase I quoted earlier, John McCloy saying we *should* "have our cake and eat it too," perfectly captures the euphoria of the imperial way of life as applied to oil. Americans, citizens as well as leaders, simply assumed that they could sell their oil abroad for a good profit while importing it from the provinces at *pennies a barrel*.

The imperial way of life was disrupted by OPEC in 1973–74. But the oil-fired empire, once symbolized by the navy and now by intercontinental bombers, could not talk about the problem in a realistic way simply because it had never come to terms with its imperial way of life. The euphemisms began to dissolve. The United States supported the creation of Israel for three reasons: a commitment to the principle of self-determination, the financial and political power of Jews in domestic American politics, and the imperial usefulness of Israel as a client state in the oil-rich Middle East. The problem was that the Palestinians also had a right to self-determined nationhood, and oil was a most effective way to make that point.

And so the crisis deepened. Kissinger said it all in one sentence: The United States must somehow "shape events in the light of our own purposes." A marvelously subtle definition of empire. But note particularly that *somehow*. What a delightful way of avoiding any coming to terms with the reality of empire. But to evade that moment of truth means again going to war.

No candor, more flight from reality. More flight, no peace. No chance finally to confront the central challenge:

Is the idea and reality of America possible without empire?

Or define the issue in these ways.

Is America *even imaginable* only on a global scale?

Are we unable, *intellectually*, to do any better than to sermonize on the theme that endless growth is crucial to our social-psychological health; and are we unable, *morally*, to share the world (say with the Palestinians as well as the Zionists) on an equitable basis?

If you answer "yes" to those questions, then hunker down for what James Baldwin once called The Fire Next Time. We will suffer what we did unto Hamburg, Dresden, and Tokyo. We will suffocate, sizzle, and fry. All in the name of defending the proposition that democracy is impossible without empire.

But consider another question. Is it possible to create and sustain a democratic culture without conquering or otherwise controlling and wasting a grossly inequitable share of social space and resources?

If you answer "yes" to *that* question then you declare yourself a pioneer on what Carl Becker might have called the ultimate American frontier. Meaning you are prepared to challenge your assumptions and join John Adams in accepting the "irksome" annoyances involved with asserting a "measure of independency."

Come along. It is certain to be more challenging than walking along the Indian trails with Daniel Boone. And surely we can do better than Jefferson or Lincoln, those heroes of the morality of having it every which way while evading the truth of empire as a way of life. It *is* time to turn in the credit cards and stop passing the buck on to the next generation.

If you are ready to bestir yourself to face that issue, we can take comfort and courage from that impressive, and delightfully variegated, group of Americans who created the tradition of speaking truth to empire. We need to stop here for a moment to avoid confusion. To be honest, History must tell

the story of those who won: why they won and how they
intended to exploit their victory. But also History must tell
us about those who offered an alternative vision and discuss
the value of their different views.

So let us think about the people who lost. Now is the time
to learn from them. Truth to tell, an impressive lot. Those
people who said *no* to empire as the only definition of democracy: a delightfully unclassifiable collection of women and
men. There are slave owners like John Taylor of Caroline
County, Quaker abolitionists from Pennsylvania, and descendants of slaves like William E. B. DuBois and A. Philip
Randolph. There are thrice-over certified conservatives such
as John Quincy Adams and Herbert Hoover. There are radicals of your choice: say Eugene Debs or the Women's League
for Peace and Freedom. And there are liberals like Robert La
Follette, Carl Becker, Charles Beard, or Helen G. Douglas.

The exciting and profoundly important thing about all of
those human beings is that they began as advocates of a system based on empire and then became, through their experience and reflection (the essence of *doing* history), people who
questioned and challenged that conventional relationship between democracy and empire.

It works, it happens, down the line. I live in a non-
academic community. You have to earn your way in. My
way is pool. I like the game and play it well. Professors playing pool with loggers and truck drivers and gippo fishermen
properly go through an apprenticeship. You beat us at our
game and we will try your game. Now my game at pool is to
play the capitalist machine tables in such a way as most
nearly to duplicate the real game of pool. No slop, no errant
ball counts. You call your shots and bank the Eight Ball. The
fascinating thing is that people like to be challenged to play
the best they can in the most difficult circumstances. *They
like the tough game.*

And that is where we are in the relationship between empire and democracy. So back to Taylor and Adams and Debs and straight pool. We come down to these questions.

1. Who makes policy on the basis of what perceptions and interests? I think here of Herbert Hoover trying to control the bankers. We have a right to know. Hoover lost in the 1920s and we have lost. *We do not know.*

2. Assume empire is necessary: what is the optimum size of the empire; and what are the proper—meaning moral as well as pragmatic—means of structuring, controlling, and defending the empire so that it will in practice produce welfare and democracy for the largest number of the imperial population?

3. What is the minimum effective size of the empire?

4. What happens if we simply say "no" to empire? Or do we have either the imagination or the courage to say "no" to empire?

It is now *our* responsibility. It has to do with how we live and how we die. We as a culture have run out of imperial games to play. Assume the worst. Empire as a way of life will lead to nuclear death. Community as a way of life will lead for a time to less than is necessary. Some of us will die. But how one dies is terribly important. It speaks to the truth of how we have lived.

CONCLUSION
Notes on Freedom Without Empire

After all, my friend, I do not at all wonder that so much reluctance has been shewn to the measure of independency. All great changes are irksome to the human mind, especially those which are attended with great dangers and uncertain effects.

JOHN ADAMS to JAMES WARREN, April 22, 1776

A war with Russia meant the extinction of Western civilization or what there was left of it. I stated I had no patience with people who formulated policies in respect to other nations "short of war." They always lead to war.

HERBERT C. HOOVER to HARRY S. TRUMAN, May 28, 1945

I don't believe for a second that the Soviets have any grand design. . . . I think it is extremely important for the U.S. to learn to walk more slowly.

High Soviet official after defecting, 1979

NOT SO VERY long ago, in 1969–70, a knowledgeable
and thoughtful man named E. A. V. Johnson, a self-defined
surviving "Professor-Bureaucrat," offered his own reflections
on empire as a way of life. He had, like one of Joseph
Conrad's heroes, gone down into the vortex of The Imperial
State and somehow reappeared on the surface with a profound *knowing* about the nature of empire: "We have been
content with pretending to do something creative, smugly
dressing up the old, tired ineffectual policies to make them
appear different and modern."*

And then, as I have done earlier in this essay, he quoted
that wise historian named Carl Becker. Becker said in pain
and sorrow—with *knowing*—that the United States "would
embark on some new variant of imperialism." Then, in part
paraphrasing Becker, Johnson spoke his experience to that insight. "There is no use dissembling, said Becker, with his
characteristic honesty; 'we might just as well call it "imperialism" and not be hypnotized or befuddled by words.' "

---

*E. A. W. Johnson, *American Imperalism in the Image of Peer Gynt: Memoirs of a
Professor-Bureaucrat* (Minneapolis: University of Minnesota Press, 1971).

Johnson was weary of all the befuddlement. Very likely depressed. He cast his memoir in an image that most citizens have not been educated to understand. (Remember Ike on education within the empire?) He chose the story of Peer Gynt, a likable sort who upon dying felt upset, frustrated and demeaned because his soul was preserved as a common bit of lead. A button. Gynt became incensed. He raged that the insult was totally unfair because he had not been "a major sinner."

"But, my friend, that precisely is your offense. You aren't a sinner in the larger sense; That's why you're let off the fiery griddle; And go, like the rest, in the casting ladle." Gynt finally understood it: he admitted that he had never given himself over to "the painful struggle to realize himself in truth and freedom." Johnson had a marvelous sense of what was happening—and not happening—in America: We were not giving ourselves over to that painful struggle; and, unless we did, we too would go into the casting ladle and come out a lead button.

This approach to history involves two kinds of activity. It begins with an honest reading of what we find in the mirror of our history, and proceeds as a continuing dialogue about how to be leaders (and to promote the common welfare) without being imperialists. It is a demanding task, no less and very probably more difficult than any of our imperial accomplishments. As John Adams knew, "all great changes are irksome to the human mind, especially those which are attended with great dangers and uncertain effects."

We can begin with the cryptic folk wisdom of Owen Bassingthwaite, a delightfully earthy Australian who supervises a mammoth ranch in the Outback. Most of the time he finds his way over several *million* square miles of open country in a Toyota pick-up. When he gets a bit befuddled, he knows how to coin a phrase. "You aren't lost until you don't know where you've been." Let us translate his insight into a form appropriate to our present predicament. Until we understand and acknowledge our imperial past, we will be lost because until then we will not know where we have been.

Very often a sympathetic friend provides crucial support when we must wind up our nerve and look straight into the mirror. Raymond Aron, a perceptive Frenchman who staunchly supported many of our imperial ventures, recently tried to provide that encouragement. Although he is deeply concerned about our imperial difficulties, he speaks most soberly about the issue: "From Yankee Imperialism to Soviet Hegemony?" Aron has a rather apocalyptic—or at any rate haunted—vision of international affairs, but he knows we need to come to terms with our Yankee Imperialism.

He begins by noting that after 1944 Americans developed an "oversimplified picture" of the world. He then speaks candidly about the way that the United States has "dominated the World Market"—"as good as reigned alone." That ultimately led to "over-confidence in [America's] technological resources"; a reference not only to Kennedy's arrogance about nuclear supremacy, but also to complacency in the face of superior electronic products, cameras, steel, and automobiles from Japan and Germany.

Aron then comments (as did Thomas Lamont many years before) on how the "ill-founded" faith in traditional gunboat diplomacy, that "simple confidence," was undone in Korea. (He could have added Cuba, where that belief was undone even more dramatically.) And, finally, he reveals how the coming together of the oil producers in OPEC was in effect a peaceful convergence of Korea, Cuba, and Vietnam. Having for so long lived and thought in "fear of revolution," the United States was not prepared to acknowledge and come to terms with the truth that the troubles were caused "not by Moscow but by the peoples concerned."

As Aron distilled the substance of this essay, so R. S.

Rajaratan, the Singapore Minister of Foreign Affairs, condensed Aron. "No single nation however big and powerful can dominate a world of some 140 interdependent nations and embracing some four billion people." The time had come to make and act upon the "important distinction between world leadership and world domination." It would be a painful process, but we must "take the risks and accept the discipline." Or, as Jason Epstein put it, it was time to define a new Americanism. It was no longer enough to find "nothing tragic in human endeavor," and no longer sufficient to ground a culture or a policy in the arrogant assumption that "evil is always external."

Such efforts to begin a serious dialogue about the limits of empire, and which alternatives to explore, quickly prompted the traditionalists to reassert the imperial outlook. Some of those people have stressed the primary importance of increased arms spending, and the reinvigoration of the will to be tough in dealing with the Soviet Union and other external evils. Others, less overtly militarily-minded, have concentrated on the need to create what George Lichtheim has described as a new interdependent world economy "controlled by a unified elite of scientifically trained managers who have left the state behind and merged their separate identities in the formation of a global cartel linking all the industrially advanced centers of the world."

It is much too simple to dismiss such rhetoric as the fantasies of the corporations organized as the Trilateral Commission or the waking dreams of those who, like Acheson, want to get a new grip on History and shape it to their purposes. We are talking about what Eisenhower correctly defined as the industrial-military-educational complex that has no conception of America except as an empire. Such people simply cannot imagine redefining foreign policy as a *means* to creating an American community. They see an imperial foreign policy as the *end* and purpose of American culture. They lack any idea of community beyond a system presided over by the United States as a benevolent policeman.

Irving Kristol, a distinguished member of the Board of Contributors to the *Wall Street Journal*, reveals the essence of that outlook with typical flair and style. "There is far too much easy and glib talk these days about the need for Americans to tighten their belts, accept a reduction in their living standards, even resign themselves to an economic philosophy of no growth. It is dangerous and irresponsible talk. . . . What few seem to realize is that a prospect of economic growth is a crucial precondition for the survival of any modern democracy, the American included." The American sense of progress hinges on the lineal projection of the imperial idea: from the British mercantilists of the 16th and 17th centuries through Franklin, Madison, and Jackson and on down to the present through Theodore Roosevelt, Woodrow Wilson, and Harry Truman.

The first thing to note is the imperial confusion of an economically defined *standard* of living with a *culturally* defined *quality* of life. Let us agree that many Americans enjoy—wallow in—a high standard of living. But no imperial statesman, Kristol included, ever provides the cost accounting to tell us what we pay for our largesse. Various others have done their best to inform us about that: say foreigners like Thucydides and Shakespeare, Americans like Melville, Charles Beard, and Carl Becker, and still others like K. William Knapp, Moses I. Finley, E. F. Schumacher, and Charles E. Lindbloom. To say nothing of Lewis Carroll. We might usefully consider Osbert Lancaster, who in *The Saracen's Head, or The Reluctant Crusader*, offered these words to ponder. "The ruins of the castle of Courantsdair were long conspicuous, but were finally sold by the father of the present Lord Littlehampton some years ago in order to pay death duties."

Whatever its benefits or rewards, empire is expensive. It costs a very great deal of money. It kills a large number of human beings. It confines and progressively throttles spontaneity and imagination. It substitutes paranoid togetherness for community. It limits the play of the mind. And even at the rudimentary marketplace level it becomes self-defeating. However unknowingly, John Locke made that point several centuries ago: The imperial satisfaction with riches, even its conception of riches, is defined not by how much we require to meet our human needs, but by how much more we acquire than our neighbors.

And so we return to oil, the classic example of the benefits and terrors of empire as a way of life. Two unusually thoughtful, concerned, and informed people reporting on the 1979 Energy Project at the Harvard Business School make my point. Robert Storbaugh and Daniel Yergin have no illusions about "an easy fix." Unlike many others, moreover, they understand that "thinking about energy raises important questions about income generation and distribution: What are the total costs and benefits involved in any decision, who profits and who pays?" Impressive, candid talk.

Well, at least up to a point. The problem is that not even a Storbaugh and a Yergin are willing to come to terms with empire as a way of life. They discount those who look that issue straight in the eye by calling them "romanticists." What an irony: The frontiersmen were once called romanticists and now the stay-at-homes are called romanticists. Or, more accurately, both are now called romanticists. It is an old and often effective ploy, intellectually and politically, but we do need to get on beyond that kind of honest cleverness.

According to Yergin and Storbaugh, one group of romantics—the "more powerful"—want to go on as usual: honoring a belief in "unlimited production and that production alone can be the nation's solution." Storbaugh and Yergin do not say so explicitly, but they are far too worldly not to know that policy based on that outlook will lead on to nuclear war and very little production. They define the other romantics as those "who have a vision of the national life decentralized . . . to the point where it becomes a post-industrial pastoral society." They are far too intelligent not to know that is a quirky evasion of a serious alternative.

The true romantics, that is to say, are those who define American culture in terms of oil. There are many such frenzied spinners of nylon in the air, or choppers-down of natural gas into artificial wood or metal—even grass. The navy and the air force also like the oozing stuff. But there is a delightful fairy tale about it all involving Henry Ford and Al Capone, told to us by F. Scott Fitzgerald.

Or perhaps it is a morality play. That is what our great American writers have always told us they were about: the definition and realization of that never produced Great American Novel. But no one, however talented (not even Melville), can write tragic novels or plays about America until we Americans confront the truth of our imperial way of life. Many fine writers have tried. Say. . . . But we all know their names. Not a few of them tell tales about private detectives. They understand we are doing our best.

Professional literary criticism, let alone intellectual history, does not get us very far across the flooded river. Let us pole our way along with Fitzgerald. He refined cars and women and men into the truth about our propensity to project the present into the future. "Can't repeat the past. . . . Why of course we can." Fitzgerald was telling us that Ford and Capone were the modern heroes we all counted on to sustain our imperial way of life. We would like to think better of ourselves, but we have yet to earn such self-respect.

And so we like Fitzgerald. He tells us an enchanting story about how the black messy guck is in truth the clean magic that brings ever more goodies and greater freedom. Embrace the greasy frog, so to speak, and the world is yours in pristine beauty. Get the oil and you got it made: have sex anywhere, rob banks anywhere, deliver booze anywhere, and shoot up the natives anywhere. All in all, oil enabled Americans to go on running away from reality. Nobody could ask for more.

Fitzgerald (and Hemingway and Pound and Eliot) knew what was going on way back then and tried to tell us before it was too late. So it simply will not do for Storbaugh and Yergin to dismiss their *knowing*—along with that of Carl Becker and Charles Beard and E. A. V. Johnson—as romantics playing under the toadstools with fairies from a "post-industrial pastoral society."

True, the people so dismissed as romantics did have a vision. They thought it possible for us Americans to transform the empire into a community. Neither Yergin nor Storbaugh has the vision or can imagine the challenge. Therein lies the true tragedy. The way that empire as a way of life kills the imagination.

Let me tell you a story, offer you a few aphorisms, and tell you another story. After all, that is the nature of an essay.

There was this man who left the Soviet Union. He knew a very great deal about policy discussions in the highest reaches of the Soviet State. We can be sure that he was turned this way and that way by our extremely competent twisters in their efforts to determine whether or not he was being planted to spy upon and influence American policy. He unwound straight, and his knowledge and intelligence were put to work in Washington. Give close attention to his judgment on two vital matters:

"I don't believe for a second that the Soviets have any grand design. . . . I think it is extremely important for the U.S. to learn to walk more slowly."

Let us consider the possibility that this man is an extremely sophisticated Soviet agent most carefully and cleverly implanted as a trusted adviser to American policy-makers. If so, how do we read his message? Is he sent to quiet us for the expansion of Russian power, or is he sent as a subtle envoy carrying the same message that Khrushchev so crudely tried to deliver in 1962 by placing missiles in Cuba? Or is he straight, and using his knowledge to warn us that our imperial policy is counter productive?

While I have no doubt that he left Moscow as his own man, I want to suggest that *it does not make any difference*. The heart of his message—"it is extremely important for the United States to learn to walk more slowly"—remains true whether one treats him as the ultimate spy, as a defector who has made a good life for himself, or as a person deeply concerned to help all of us get on with the labor of creating a more humane life.

If he is the spy of spies, that is to say, then clearly his purpose is to encourage us to relax while Russia replaces us as the superior imperial power. Given our recent experience we do not stand to lose much by that: a rational conception of American security—economic or military—does not depend upon the kind of global superiority that the United States has enjoyed since 1945. Let the Russians waste their resources, fight and lose those provincial wars, and in the process destabilize their precariously balanced political economy. We can get on with important matters.

If he is trying to help us do that because he believes that we have the best chance of imagining and creating a better way of life, then we come out with the same policy. Get on with important matters. Turn away from empire and begin to create a community. At the very least we must break free of the paranoia that defines all our problems as caused by external evil.

I have no list of answers. Only a fool unrolls blueprints and specifications for changing a way of life. In any event, none of us has thought about it long and seriously enough to offer even a serious set of possible alternatives. But I do have these suggestions about basic points of reference—or a perspective.

We can begin with Sir Francis Burton.

"Indeed he knows not how to know who knows not also how to un-know."

Then in the idiom of the marketplace, listen to Miguel de Cervantes.

"Make it thy business to know thyself, which is the most difficult lesson in the world."

And, next to last, Pilpay.

"We ought to do our neighbor all the good we can. If you do good, good will be done to you; but if you do evil, the same will be measured back to you again."

Finally, give up the conception of human existence defined by the standard of living for one that is grounded in the quality of life.

It is a slow and painful way to learn, this imperial burning of finger after finger to find out that the stove is hot. Let us save our thumbs to grasp a non-imperial future.

Some pages back I spoke very seriously about the visceral importance of admitting that we Americans devised and benefited from an imperial way of life. So let me tell you a story about what I mean by coming to terms with the truth.

The moral of the tale has nothing to do with being soft on communism or unilateral disarmament or pacifism. We, all of us, here and elsewhere, are in a transition period that offers us the opportunity to imagine and act upon a way to move on beyond global imperialism to regional communities. Away from the kind of interdependence programmed by the computers of the multinational corporations to the kind of dialogue that is the substance of a neighborhood.

Thus the point of the story involves the development and acceptance, and the honoring in practice of humanely responsible expectations and limits in our relationships with each other. It speaks to the necessity of creating an alternative to empire as a way of life, and then of living our individual and collective lives within that more demanding and rewarding framework. We as specific human beings must confront the issue, make our choice, and act.

I was born in 1921, in the midst of a postwar depression. I came to adolescence during the Great Depression. We were not dirt poor. We were not starving, and we were not lacking the rudiments of food or clothing. But we did miss much of the rest of the so-called American Way of Life. Even so, we all believed in that American Way of Life.

That Truth was somewhere out on the back forty, or down the line. But the imperial ethos does not teach one to wait. It informs one with the assumption that the goodies should be here and now—and forever. And so I stole a very fine and expensive knife from the best hardware store in town.

My maternal grandmother, Maude Hammond Appleman, discovered what I had done. She confronted me with the question: did you steal the knife? Yes, I stole the knife. Why? Because I wanted it, because I liked it, because I can use it.

She said: the knife is not yours. You have not earned it. You will take it back.

I said: I *can't* do that.

She said: You *will* do that. *Now*.

Oh, my: the moral force of the declarative sentence.

And so I walked back along those long and lonely blocks to the store. And in through the door. And up, face to face, with the member of that small community who owned the store. And I said: I stole this knife and I am sorry and I am bringing it back.

And he said: Thank you. The knife is not very important, but you coming down here and saying that to me is very important.

Remembering all that, I know why I do not want the empire. There are better ways to live and there are better ways to die.